FILM

The 50 most influential film-makers in the world

First published in Great Britain in 2009

A & C Black Publishers Ltd
36 Soho Square
London W1D 3QY
www.acblack.com

ISBN 978 1 408 10940 3

Conceived and produced by
Elwin Street Limited
144 Liverpool Road
London N1 1LA
United Kingdom
www.elwinstreet.com

Designer: Thomas Keenes

Picture credits: All images supplied by The Kobal Collection: p. 9 (Wark Producing
Company); p. 14 (Prana-film); p. 16 (Goskino); p. 19 (UFA); pp. 22, (20th Century Fox);
pp. 24, 107 (Paramount); pp. 29, 45 (RKO); p. 31 (Columbia); pp. 39, 112 (United Artists);
p. 43, 115 (Warner Bros.); p. 55 (UA/Lions Gate); p. 56 (Societe Generale de Films); p. 59
(Nouvelle Edition Francaise); p. 63 (DAIEI); p. 65 (Greenwich); p. 71 (Sveva/Italia/Junior);
p. 74 (Toho); p. 77 (photographer: Bob Hawkins); p. 80 (Cinematograph AB Sweden/
Cinema 5); p. 83 (Rama-Pathe); p. 85 (Priya); p. 89 (Rome-Paris/De Laurentiis/
Beauregard); p. 91 (OPERA/RAI-2/SOVIN); p. 93 (Planet-film/Albatross/Gaumont); p. 95
(CAB/FR3/Canal +); p. 97 (Institute for the Intellectual Development of Children and
Young Adults); p. 100 (Jet Tone); p. 103 (Hu Tong Comm/Radiant); p. 111 (Warner Bros.,
photographer: Andrew Cooper); pp. 116, 125 (Universal); p. 121 (Bender/Spink); p. 123
(Afi/Libra); p. 127 (A Band Apart/Miramax, photographer: Andrew Cooper).

A CIP catalogue record for this book is available from the British Library.

Printed in Singapore

FILM

The 50 most influential film-makers in the world

TOM CHARITY

CONTENTS

The Masters

Modern Americans

INTRODUCTION

**Louis Lumière, the man who invented the *cinématographe*
(along with his brother Auguste), pronounced their machine
'an invention without a future'. That was in 1894. More than
a hundred years on, this novelty attraction is still going
strong in almost every corner of the globe, both as a billion-
dollar industry and an international art form. Yet film itself –
in the sense of strips of celluloid pulled through a shutter to
be exposed to the light – may finally be on the way out as the
industry gets to grips with a digital revolution that is changing
how films are shot, edited, distributed and screened.**

This is not a bad time, then, to look back and take stock of the
most significant achievements in the first century of cinema.
'The task I am trying to achieve is above all to make you see', silent-
film pioneer, D W Griffith, once said. Some might counter that we've
seen too much and understood too little, but there's no question that
moving pictures have transformed our knowledge of the world, the
way we see ourselves and relate to others. They have influenced every
aspect of our lives, from war and politics to fashion and design, and
even standards of private and public morality.

For a relatively young art form, film has developed in myriad
directions, encompassing documentary and animation, realism and
fantasy, pornography and propaganda. Even so, narrative film quickly
became the dominant popular mode, and despite some significant
local variations the fundamental syntax of classical film grammar was
in place by the time that sound film took hold in the late 1920s.

That dominance is reflected in the selection of 50 film-makers
that feature in this book. So, too, is the ubiquity of American movies
throughout most parts of the world (India and parts of Asia excepted).
Roughly half of these people worked mostly in, or around, Hollywood.

The other half takes us to Japan, India, the Soviet Union, Iran, Hong Kong, China and, of course, across the length and breadth of Europe.

This is not to say that Africa, Australasia and South America have not produced great film-makers – it would be easy to press a claim for Ousmane Sembene, Jane Campion or Glauber Rocha, to cite just three examples. The 50 who did make the final cut were chosen on the strength of technical innovation and influence, historical importance and artistic excellence. Taken together – and with ten essays to fill in some of the gaps – they map a broad outline for a history of the cinema, and point the way towards further exploration and discovery.

The notion of the film director as artist is, itself, an outmoded concept in some academic circles. To be sure, 'auteurism' is only one approach to cinema, and it is important to recognise that this is a collaborative art, a commercial industry and a language system that can be decoded through all manner of sciences. Nevertheless, as a rule, the director works longer on a film than anyone else, and in the widest capacity. And there is no doubt that the film-makers in this book were all creative and resourceful artists who channelled themselves and their times into wonderful shadows that danced upon the screen.

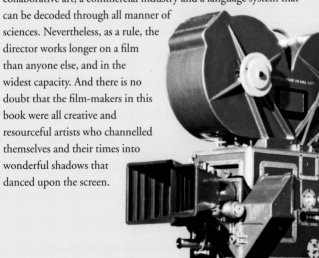

David Wark Griffith

D W Griffith was the pre-eminent American director of the pre-First World War era, among the first to appreciate the artistic potential of the medium. An innovator, he melded much of what we understand to be the language of narrative film. In the epics *The Birth of a Nation* and *Intolerance,* he laid the foundations for the Hollywood feature film.

Born 1875, La Grange, Kentucky, United States
Importance Founding father of American narrative film
Died 1948, Los Angeles, California, United States

Griffith's standing in the history of cinema is tarnished by the overt racism of his most famous accomplishment, *The Birth of a Nation* (1915), a Civil War and Reconstruction drama that valorises the Ku Klux Klan and expresses a deep dread of racial interbreeding. Griffith was surprised by the controversy that attached itself to America's first feature-length film even before it had been released, but the three-hour melodrama was a tremendous financial success, and was endorsed by President Woodrow Wilson, who pronounced it as 'history writ with lightning'.

The monumental scale of this film and its even more ambitious successor, *Intolerance* (1916) was inspired, in large part, by Italian epics such as *Quo Vadis?* (1912) and *Cabiria* (1914), but it is important to recognise that Griffith's contribution to the development of film syntax goes deeper than these grand spectacles.

During his six years at the Biograph company, 1907 to 1913, the actor and aspiring playwright began to direct and, together with cameraman Billy Bitzer, brought a new range of expressive techniques to the 'photoplay', including a far more nuanced juxtaposition of long, medium and close shots, fade-outs as a visual punctuation mark, panning camera moves, and cross-cutting between discrete actions to generate suspense. Griffith was not the only film-maker to experiment with these devices, but in more than 400 one-reelers (each about 12 to 14 minutes long) he and Bitzer effectively synthesised them into a fluid cinematic grammar.

Griffith realised that composition and montage relieved the onus on the actors. In place of the histrionic style that dominated performance in cinema's first decade, he pioneered a more restrained, realistic approach (actors who appeared in his Biograph films include Lillian and Dorothy Gish, Mary Pickford, Lionel Barrymore and Harry Carey, all of whom would enjoy significant careers until the sound era, and in some cases beyond).

The relative commercial failure of *Intolerance* forced Griffith to concentrate on less grandiose productions – and many critics prefer the simpler, more lyrical melodramas that followed: *Broken Blossoms* (1919), *Way Down East* (1920) and *Orphans of the Storm* (1921). Always cavalier

Griffith was a co-founder of United Artists in 1919 along with Mary Pickford, Douglas Fairbanks and Charlie Chaplin.

with money, and insistent on his own creative freedom, Griffith failed to capitalise on his successes and, as the 1920s progressed, he struggled to keep up with the next generation of film poets. Although his 1931 sound film, *Abraham Lincoln* was highly regarded, it was another commercial failure, and he retired soon afterwards.

Charlie Chaplin

For more than a decade, Charlie Chaplin was not just the most popular star in Hollywood, he was revered across the globe. As a clown, he brought unique grace and pathos to slapstick comedy, as well as extraordinary invention and ingenuity. As a film-maker, he was able to insist on complete autonomy.

Born 1889, London, England
Importance Iconic comedic actor and film-maker; the first international superstar
Died 1977, Vevey, Switzerland

The figure of the tramp, Chaplin's 'Little Fellow' remains a potent icon to generations who have only the faintest acquaintance with his films: the black bowler hat perched over curly hair; the jacket too tight even for his skinny frame, but buttoned once for good form's sake; trousers long and baggy, tied about the waist with string; delicate white gloves; a dandy's moustache and cane.

It is the costume of a man in straightened circumstance with aspirations to gentility – and it is immediately ridiculous. Yet Chaplin turns our scorn on its head. Through his innate decorum, his optimism, endurance and his, often mischievous, ingenuity, this perennial underdog has the last laugh. He is pathetic in the true sense of the word: he commands our pity and compassion. At the fade-out he is always alone, and we love him dearly for it.

Chaplin was an exacting director, known for doing takes over and over again until he got the perfect scene.

To modern eyes, Chaplin is sentimental, even winsome, and one could complain that he only fed his narcissism with our empathy. His childhood suggests where that overweening need came from. Both parents were in music hall (he made his stage debut at five) but his father abandoned his mother when Charlie was three, and died from alcoholism in 1901. His mother struggled with mental illness and was confined to an asylum when Charlie was still a child. He and his brother Sidney were subsequently sent to an orphanage.

In 1906, Chaplin joined Fred Karno's theatrical troupe. When the Karno company toured the US in 1913, he was spotted by Mack Sennett. In his second film for Sennett's Keystone company, *Kid Auto Races at Venice* (1914), Chaplin casually picked out the props and costume that came to define him. Within months he directed his first one-reeler and, by 1915, he was able to sign for the Essenay Company for the staggering salary of $1,250 a week (plus a $10,000 signing fee).

> **MISE-EN-SCÈNE**
> Originally a theatre term, this literally means 'put in the scene'. In filmic terms it refers to everything in front of the camera – staging, lighting, movement, design and composition.

In terms of mise-en-scène Chaplin made a virtue of simplicity. His staging remained overshadowed by the Proscenium Arch and, in the 1920s, he would be surpassed in camera technique by Buster Keaton. But he imposed his poetic sensibility through sheer force of personality. His films were markedly slower than the typical Keystone style. He gave himself more close ups; crucially, he used mime to express a finer range of emotion than any actor before him.

By 1919, Chaplin enjoyed complete creative control over his work. The films got longer – *The Kid* was his first feature, in 1921, and the most successful release since *The Birth of a Nation* – and so did the time he spent on them. For some critics he never surpassed the two-reelers from the 1917 to 1918 period that culminated in *The Immigrant*. But *The Gold Rush* (1925), *The Circus* (1928) and *City Lights* (the last great silent film, from 1931) are worthy of his renown, and at least four of six sound films are also of interest: *Modern Times* (1936), *The Great Dictator* (1940), *Monsieur Verdoux* (1947) and *Limelight* (1952), with Buster Keaton.

SILENT CINEMA

The first 30 years of cinema witnessed incomparable innovation and artistry. It conjured up the basic visual syntax of moving pictures and gave us some of the funniest and the most poignant films ever made. It established many genres that prevail to this day (see page 72), experimented with widescreen and colour and laid the foundations of the Hollywood industry. It is estimated that more than 80 per cent of the films from this period have been lost.

The cinema dates back to the 1890s, when several scientists in different countries patented their own moving-picture machines. In the US, Thomas Edison's Kinetoscope was a penny-arcade machine – the first Kinetoscope parlour opened on Broadway in 1894 promising 'The Souvenir Strip'.

In France the Lumière brothers, Louis and Auguste, unveiled their *Cinématographe* in 1895, a machine that combined camera, projector and printer all in one. Their films ran less than a minute, and offered fixed, single shots of everyday subjects: the workers leaving the Lumière factory; or a train pulling into a station. The Lumières also made the first comedy: a gardener inadvertently dousing himself with his own hose. Their programme proved so popular that, in 1896, they transferred it from the basement room of a Parisian cafe into a much larger venue, which they named the 'Cinéma Lumière'.

Magician Georges Melies tried to buy the Lumières' invention. When they refused, he built his own, constructed a glass studio in the grounds of his home in Montreuil, and went on to write, direct, photograph and act in some 500 films between 1896 and 1913. He is most famous for *Voyage to the Moon* (1902), a 14-minute science fantasy combining live action, animated and optical special effects, and hand-tinted colour frames. Melies' innovations also included stop-motion and double-exposure effects, dissolves, fades and time-lapse photography. Yet he never grasped the potential of the cut to draw us into the action; his camera remains stuck outside the theatre's invisible fourth wall.

Over the next two decades, film-makers became ever more ambitious, especially as audiences seemed to hunger for longer and more expressive pictures. In 1924, Erich von Stroheim attempted to film Frank Norris's gold rush novel *McTeague* in its entirety, on the actual San Francisco and Death Valley locations Norris described. The director's cut ran more than nine hours – but only a handful of MGM executives ever saw it. They released the film – *Greed* – in a two-hour version and melted down most of the excised footage to recover the silver nitrate. Even in this truncated form the movie's poetry remains potent.

In 1927, Abel Gance made *Napoleon*, which expended more than six hours to take Bonaparte from childhood to the brink of his Italian campaign. Despite the length, Gance's camerawork has a dynamic verve that is positively giddy, and the finale stretches the screen to accommodate 'Polyvision', a triptych that anticipated the widescreen processes of the 1950s.

This same year produced Lang's *Metropolis*, Murnau's *Sunrise*, Buster Keaton's *The General*, and Al Jolson in *The Jazz Singer* – an undistinguished melodrama save for the fact that Warner Bros decided to experiment with a synchronous sound process during half a dozen musical numbers. The movie proved such a hit that the

> 'All I need to make a comedy is a park, a policeman and a pretty girl.'
>
> Charlie Chaplin

entire industry was recalibrated for sound, and save for a handful of hangers-on, the silent film was pretty much consigned to history before the decade was out.

Friedrich Wilhelm Murnau

Arguably the consummate director of the silent era, F W Murnau created the iconic expressionist nightmare *Nosferatu* (1922) and the fantasy *Faust* (1926); an eloquent modern parable in *The Last Laugh* (*Der Letzte Mann*, 1924); and prefigured film noir in the transcendent love story *Sunrise* (1927). Murnau brought unparalleled visual sophistication to motion pictures.

Born 1888, Bielefeld, Germany
Importance A master of the silent film
Died 1931, Santa Barbara, California, United States

Murnau was schooled in art history and sometimes modelled his compositions on specific paintings. Like other German film-makers of the First World War era, he was influenced by the lighting and staging techniques of Max Reinhardt (he was part of Reinhardt's company for a time), and embraced the expressionist effects of chiaroscuro and distorted perspectives. But more importantly, Murnau made the leap to re-imagine space in terms of the mobile camera; his films have a fluidity and dynamism that still feels modern to this day.

An aviator during the First World War, Murnau formed a film company with the actor Conrad Veidt in 1919. Of his 21 films, nine are lost. But *Nosferatu* (subtitled: 'A

Vampire horror film Nosferatu *(1922) is Murnau's most famous work.*

Symphony of Horror') is among the best known of all silent films. The first, albeit unofficial, adaptation of Bram Stoker's novel *Dracula*, the film differs markedly from subsequent versions in its vivid portrait of the vampire as a ghoulish fiend with rodent-like teeth, digits and ears. Played by the tall, skeletal Max Schrek, he preys in the shadows, and merges with the darkness. If this is a creature of the expressionist imagination, *Nosferatu* stands out for Murnau's decision to film on location in medieval Baltic towns; the horror derives its special frisson from placing the supernatural within the natural world.

Faust, on the other hand, is a studio construct through and through, a fantasy film composed in every detail. Although contemporary critics were justified to complain it was a vulgarisation of Goethe, the film's imagery is often spellbinding. Critics of the 1920s preferred *The Last Laugh*, a sentimental anecdote about a proud hotel doorman (Emil Jannings) demoted to lavatory attendant when he gets too old to carry the heavy luggage. If the story is thin, Murnau's treatment was revelatory: he dispensed with intertitles altogether, and 'unchained' the camera to relate everything through his highly mobile images (including some extraordinary subjective camera episodes). Murnau's fluent articulation of expressionist devices such as superimposition, camera angle and, especially, travelling shots, all in a naturalistic drama, proved an international sensation, and he was soon offered a Hollywood contract with Twentieth Century Fox.

The first fruit of that contract was *Sunrise*. Again, Murnau chose a musical subtitle for the film: 'A Song of Two Humans', and again, the story could be described as slight: a villager is seduced by a city vamp, and comes to the brink of murdering his wife before he finds redemption. Murnau's virtuoso technique doesn't dress up the material; rather, his sublime images are the heart and soul of this essential film.

Tragically Murnau died in a car accident at the age of 42, but not before he had made *Tabu* (1931), a fascinating late silent filmed in Polynesia, with initial input from the documentarist, Robert Flaherty.

Sergei Eisenstein

Cinema's first radical formalist, Sergei Eisenstein sought a revolutionary aesthetic infused with the ideas and ideals of the new communist era. His first three films – *Strike!* (1924); *The Battleship Potemkin* (1925) and *October* (1927) – chronicle the roots and eventual triumph of the Russian Revolution, melding historical dramatisation with a powerful new dialectic constructed through bold imagery and Eisenstein's much quoted theories of montage.

Born 1898, Riga, Latvia
Importance Introduced the concept of 'an intellectual montage'
Died 1948, Moscow, Russia

In 1918 Eisenstein volunteered to serve in the Red Army and, in 1920, he joined the Workers' Theatre of Prolekult as a designer. Subsequently he worked with Visevolod Meyerhold's famous avant-garde company. In 1923 he wrote a manifesto, *The Montage of Attractions*, which developed Lev Kuleshov's ideas about the construction of meaning through editing. Throughout his career, Eisenstein would return to his concept of 'an intellectual montage', in which counterpoint and juxtaposition produce not just a visceral reaction, but a distinct political reading. There is an especially stark example in

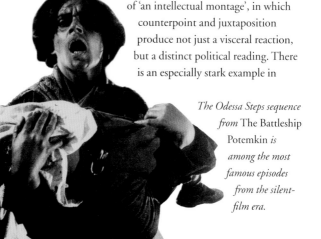

The Odessa Steps sequence from The Battleship Potemkin *is among the most famous episodes from the silent-film era.*

Strike!, when shots of the police assaulting workers are cut with brutal footage from a slaughterhouse.

If the propaganda sounds simplistic, Eisenstein's genius lay in his gift for building momentum through contrapuntal rhythm, a facility that allowed him to dispense with the conventional bourgeois narrative of the solitary hero. His films from the 1920s contained six times as many edits as the norm (scholars have calculated an Average Shot Length, ASL, of just two seconds for *October*).

The Battleship Potemkin (a recreation of a 1905 incident when sailors mutinied against their Tsarist officers) was judged a real threat to Western capitalism and the film was banned in Britain until 1954 and in Spain, France and Nazi Germany. The film exerted an enormous influence on cinephiles around the world.

Eisenstein's preoccupation with montage did not come out of nowhere. There are obvious parallels with the dynamic effects modern artists were exploring in constructivism and cubism. By 1923, the Russian film-maker Dziga Vertov was already experimenting with an audacious cinematic cut-up technique in his *Kino-Eye* newsreels. (Eisenstein preferred what he called 'Kino-Fist'.) And he wasn't simply an inspired editor; his meticulously pre-planned compositions are angular and expressionist, and he makes liberal use of visual shorthand, symbolism and caricature.

MONTAGE
Initially used in connection with Russian theories about intellectual editing, this term came to refer to all editing in general, as well as to describe short, heavily-edited interludes and any sequence where the editing serves a rhetorical purpose, as opposed to the 'invisible' continuity editing of the classic Hollywood film.

Sent off on an international tour by his government sponsors, Eisenstein arrived in Hollywood in 1930, but a plan to film Theodore Dreiser's *American Tragedy* proved too radical for Paramount, and a Mexican project was also abandoned. When Eisenstein returned to Russia, he was no longer the regime's favourite son. *Alexander Nevsky* (1936) was a stirring propaganda epic, but its nationalist tub-thumping marked an intellectual retreat. The controversial *Ivan the Terrible* was planned as a trilogy, but Eisenstein only completed the first two parts (1944 and 1946) before his death.

Architect of Film Noir

Fritz Lang

**A seminal director in at least two genres – the fantasy film
and film noir – and in two very different film industries, Fritz
Lang is one of the prime case studies of the auteur theory (see
Auteurism, page 26). Whatever their provenance,
Lang's pictures all share a grim apprehension that
man is alone in his struggles against an uncaring
or malevolent fate.**

Born 1890, Vienna,
Austria
Importance A
prominent film-maker
in both Germany and
Hollywood, famous for
noir melodramas
Died 1976, Los Angeles,
California, United States

Lang had two quite separate careers: he was the pre-
eminent film-maker in Germany between the wars
(an epoch that gave us Murnau, Pabst and Lubitsch),
producing widely popular, lavish spectacles like *Die
Nibelungen* (1924) and the seminal fantasy film,
Metropolis (1927). Then, for 20 years, he plied his
trade as a Hollywood studio director, specialising for the most part in
spare, production-line thrillers, largely overlooked by both critics and
peers. Yet today, his American movies are the cornerstone of his
reputation as one of the most rigorous and intelligent of film-makers.

Metropolis is undoubtedly his most famous and influential film,
although we are still piecing together the true nature of its
achievement 80 years after it premiered in a 153-minute version that
was drastically truncated to less than 90 minutes (in 2008 several
'lost' scenes were rediscovered in Argentina). A mytho-prophetic
nightmare of industrial society, the film imagines a decadent elite
thriving on the exploitation of an oppressed underclass and remains
astonishing for its towering visual imagination.

The sprawling *Dr Mabuse, the Gambler* (1922) was another
landmark, most notable for its eponymous arch villain, a criminal
mastermind who hypnotises his marks, and in whom critics detect
foreshadows of Adolf Hitler. But Lang's greatest film from this period

is his first sound film, *M* (1931), an expressionist masterpiece about a child murderer pursued through the streets of Dusseldorf. Lorre's pitiable cry, 'I can't help myself,' carries an existential horror that runs through almost all of Lang's subsequent work in America.

Lang excelled at noir melodramas, stripping away appearances to expose deeper and darker truths that society prefers not to acknowledge. *The Woman in the Window* (1944) and *Scarlet Street* (1945) stand out.

After a brief flirtation with baroque atmospherics, in the 1950s Lang refined and pared down his mise-en-scène to the elementals, a kind of backlot purgatory where flat, solid unremarkable men (Glenn Ford; Dana Andrews) succumb

Lang's Metropolis *captivated viewers with its bleak vision of the future.*

to forces greater than themselves. It's not that they can't exercise free will, but they remain trapped in a pattern of remorseless logic that allows for precious little grace. *The Big Heat* (1953) – about a cop's crazed vendetta against the mob that controls his city and murdered his wife – is about as upbeat as Lang gets. After the pulp Kafka of *Beyond a Reasonable Doubt* (1956) Lang quit the US, made three defiantly personal films in India and Germany, then appeared as himself in Godard's *Le mépris* (1963).

Ernst Lubitsch

One of the first European directors to be imported by Hollywood, Ernst Lubitsch fashioned the comedy of manners with a cosmopolitan sophistication and wit that inspired many of the finest films of Hollywood's so-called 'Golden Age' (circa 1920 to 1947).

Born 1892, Berlin, Germany
Importance Replaced traditional slapstick with a new, subtler approach to comedy
Died 1947, Los Angeles, California, United States

Film comedy in the 1920s was dominated by the slapstick pioneered by Mack Sennett and Hal Roach: Chaplin, Buster Keaton, Harold Lloyd, Fatty Arbuckle, Harry Langdon, Charley Chase, et al. A student of Max Reinhardt, Lubitsch certainly wasn't above physical comedy but, as a director, he drew on theatrical models, farce, operetta and the drawing room comedy, conventions of gender reversal, mistaken identity, infidelity and imposture that date back at least as far as Shakespeare.

Lubitsch enjoyed his biggest successes with romantic comedies and lavish historical dramas like *Madame Dubarry* (1919) and *Anna Boleyn* (1920). He was particularly renowned for his collaborations with actresses Pola Negri and Ossi Oswalda ('the German Mary Pickford'), and it was Pickford who invited him

Lubitsch directed three dozen pictures between 1915 and 1923.

to come to Hollywood. He was accepted almost immediately. His second film, *The Marriage Circle* (1924), was much admired by contemporary critics for its simplicity and naturalism, its 'Continental character' and 'subtlety of humour'.

'I let the audience use their imaginations. Can I help it if they misconstrue my suggestions?'

Sex is central to Lubitsch's appeal. Americans attributed his casual, debonair eroticism to European sophistication (most of his films were set in a fanciful Old Europe), although Hollywood in the Jazz Age was probably as decadent as anywhere at the time. In *Three Women* (1924), *Kiss Me Again, Lady Windemere's Fan* (both 1925) and *So This is Paris* (1926) Lubitsch refined an enchantingly elegant notion of the high life, an emancipated realm where desire and deceit go hand in hand with discretion and decorum.

Unlike the slapstick giants, Lubitsch lost nothing in the transition to sound. *The Love Parade* (1929) started a series of cheeky operettas for Paramount starring Maurice Chevalier and Jeanette MacDonald. The studio was so impressed it made Lubitsch Head of Production.

In 1934, Joseph Breen of the Hollywood Production Code (which monitored studio films for breaches in taste) tried to impose a puritanical morality on American pictures that sought to neuter the candour of sex comedies like *Trouble in Paradise* (1932). But the sly innuendos and subversive strategies of screwball comedy were already embedded in Lubitsch's taste for insinuation and implication. After all, the charm of the famous 'Lubitsch Touch' hinges on its subtlety and understatement, as well as its inherent romance. *The Shop Around the Corner* (1940) is a silly trifle invested with such grace and feeling that it may be the finest romantic comedy ever made.

Ninotchka (1939) was another triumph, a defiant celebration of hedonism at the expense of socialism. *To Be Or Not To Be* (1942) imagined that a second-rate theatre troupe could put one over on the Third Reich, and in *Heaven Can Wait* (1943) the Devil himself gets the runaround from an unrepentant roué.

John Ford

If one had to nominate a poet laureate from Hollywood's 'Golden Age', then John Ford would be that man. His work traverses six decades of American cinema, more than 100 films, dramas, literary adaptations, comedies, war films and melodramas – yet he remains indivisibly associated with the western, the genre he elevated to its highest expression.

Born 1894, Cape Elizabeth, Maine, United States
Importance A top film director, famous for westerns
Died 1973, Palm Desert, California, United States

A proud and contrary Irish-American, born Sean O'Fearna, Ford travelled West before the dust had settled on the frontier and arrived in Hollywood in time to play a Klansman in D W Griffith's *The Birth of a Nation* (1915). He started directing in 1917, and produced two-dozen popular, unpretentious westerns with Harry Carey, before turning his hand to the transcontinental railway epic *The Iron Horse* (1924). By the end of the silent era, Ford was one of the top directors at Fox, prized for his versatility and efficiency as much as his artistry.

His reputation rose steeply with *The Informer* (1935); self-consciously arty expressionism built around Victor McLaglen's blustery performance as a tragic IRA goon. The film won four Academy Awards, including the first of Ford's four Best

Darryl F. Zanuck presents
JOHN FORD'S
MY DARLING CLEMENTINE
HENRY FONDA · LINDA DARNELL · VICTOR MATURE
WALTER BRENNAN
TIM HOLT
CATHY DOWNS
DIRECTED BY JOHN FORD
PRODUCED BY SAMUEL G. ENGEL
20TH CENTURY-FOX

One of the greatest classic westerns of all time, My Darling Clementine *(1946) was filmed in just over 45 days.*

Director statuettes. Fortunately, Ford rarely indulged his artistic bent to this extent; *The Informer*, *The Long Voyage Home* (1940) and *The Fugitive* (1947) stand as intriguing anomalies, evidence of a suffocating admiration for Murnau and Eisenstein. He is more himself in a piece of folksy Southern nostalgia like *Steamboat Round the Bend* (1935), one of three comedies he made with Will Rogers.

Most famously, of course, there are the westerns: he restored adult credibility to the brand in 1939 with *Stagecoach*, his first sound western, and the first to put John Wayne in Monument Valley. *My Darling Clementine* (1946); *She Wore a Yellow Ribbon* (1949); *Wagonmaster* (1950); *The Searchers* (1956); and *The Man Who Shot Liberty Valance* (1962) are central to any discussion of the genre.

Certainly, Ford was an elegist and a myth-monger, not a historian, but he was also more complex than he let on. He may have subscribed to Manifest Destiny, but he was also acutely sensitive to what was sacrificed with the advance of 'civilisation'; the passing of the old before the new (see also, in a completely different context, *How Green Was My Valley*, 1941).

Ford can be criticised for lackadaisical buffoonery and egregious sentimentality. For all that he railed against studio interference and 'cut in the camera',

MANIFEST DESTINY
First voiced by expansionist US politicians in the 1840s, this was the principle that declared 'Americans' had a divine duty to spread freedom and democracy across the land (expressing no respect for those whom they saw as the 'savages' who stood in their way).

giving studio editors no option but to follow his shot plan, some of his best work is indebted to the shrewd overview of Fox head Darryl F Zanuck – especially the classic John Steinbeck adaptation *The Grapes of Wrath* (1940). As the studio system declined so, too, did the quality of his output.

Nevertheless, Zanuck would be the first to allow that Ford was more than a superb craftsman. In many ways he epitomises the classical tradition in American film, and certainly he represents an important bridge between the visual poetry of silent-picture making and the pragmatism of the production line.

Alfred Hitchcock

Alfred Hitchcock was probably the most famous director of the mid-twentieth century. In a career that stretched from the silent era to the 1970s, he directed more than 50 films and rarely strayed from his favourite genre, the suspense thriller. His success allowed him to develop a unique style and delve into personal obsessions within the framework of popular entertainment.

Born 1899, London, England
Importance Directed many successful suspense thrillers
Died 1980, Bel Air, California, United States

A devout Catholic, Hitchcock often attributed his fascination with – and fear of – transgression and punishment to an episode in his childhood when his parents escorted him to the local police station and asked the sergeant to lock him up. The story may be apocryphal, but there is palpable repression and dread in Hitchcock's superficially insouciant cinema.

A gifted artist, Hitchcock found work designing intertitles for silent films, and was a screenwriter, art director and assistant director before he made his first film, *The Pleasure*

Hitchcock was famous for talking about 'the MacGuffin', a plot motor that drives the story, but is of no consequence to the audience – like the money Marion steals in Psycho *(1960), but which Norman Bates never discovered.*

Garden, in Munich in 1925. In Germany, he came under the influence of expressionists like Lang and Murnau, and was also introduced to Eisenstein's theories of montage (page 17). Hitchcock fused these aesthetics with his own ideas about manipulation and the mechanics of suspense. More than any director in Hollywood, he wrote in moving images, often to the consternation of his screenwriters, who had the task of weaving his visual conceits into a coherent narrative.

Among his films of the 1920s and 1930s, *Blackmail* (1929) was the first British sound picture, and an exhilarating demonstration of the possibilities it opened up. *The 39 Steps* (1935) and *The Lady Vanishes* (1938) are spry, witty thrillers, and templates for more fun and games in later entertainments.

By 1939, when producer David O Selznick lured him to Hollywood, Hitchcock's motifs were well established, including his predilection for blondes in peril and for innocent protagonists who find themselves in the wrong place at the wrong time.

Hitchcock claimed no interest in character or psychology and shrugged off deeper interpretation of his themes. He was famous for meticulously storyboarding every frame of his films in advance. He seemed disinterested on set and claimed 'actors should be treated like cattle'. Nevertheless he insisted on prime beef: Cary Grant, James Stewart, Ingrid Bergman and Grace Kelly were among his favourites.

Shadow of a Doubt (1943), *Notorious* (1946) and *Strangers on a Train* (1951) are all first-rate examples of his art. But Hitchcock hit his peak in the mid-to-late 1950s with a string of masterpieces: *Rear Window*, *The Wrong Man*, *Vertigo*, *North by Northwest* and then *Psycho* and *The Birds*. By now the French critics were analysing his work with a reverence that dismayed their counterparts in the English-speaking world, who had always taken him at face value, as a jovial entertainer, a showman. His oeuvre became perhaps the most debated test case for auteurism (see page 26), and later proved just as fascinating to structuralist and feminist theorists.

AUTEURISM

**If film is an art form, then surely it requires an artist?
Developed in France after the Second World War, auteurist
criticism installed the director as the 'author' of a film in the
same way that a composer authors a symphony. Auteurism
gradually gained acceptance in the English-speaking world,
although it now survives in a heavily modified form.**

In the mid-twentieth century, cinema was still struggling to
establish its credentials as an art form, as opposed to an industrial
entertainment that sometimes came dressed up in the borrowed
clothes of more prestigious literary and dramatic forms. The *'politique
des auteurs'* as framed by the critics at *Cahiers du Cinéma* magazine in
the 1950s was, in large part, a polemic attack on this conservative
tradition of quality at the heart of French film-making, the *'cinéma
du papa'*, as the Young Turks called it.

Of course, outstanding, uncompromising film-makers like
Chaplin and Lubitsch had long been recognised as artists in their own
right, but the auteurists extended that claim to those production-line
directors in Hollywood whose work had previously been patronised
or overlooked.

The term *politique des auteurs* was coined by François Truffaut in
the pages of *Cahiers du Cinéma*
in 1954. He was building on
the formalist criticism of the
magazine's founder, André Bazin,
and a 1948 essay by Alexandre
Astruc, who came up with the
idea of the *'caméra-stylo'*: the
camera as a director's pen. In this light, the received literary qualities
of a screenplay are subservient to the alchemical processes of mise-en-

> *'A film is never really good
> unless the camera is an eye
> in the head of a poet.'*
>
> Orson Welles

scène (see page 11), which would include shot composition and duration, staging, decor, lighting and performance.

Truffaut and his colleagues – including future French new-wave luminaries like Jean-Luc Godard, Jacques Rivette, Eric Rohmer and Claude Chabrol – constructed a new critical canon to celebrate these visionary auteurs. Many of them were American and working in popular cinema. At the top of pile was Orson Welles, then came Howard Hawks, John Ford, Nicholas Ray and Alfred Hitchcock (his English films were given short shrift), but they also championed numerous B-movie directors, like Edgar G Ulmer, Joseph H Lewis and Allan Dwan.

By establishing the director as the true creative force, not the writer or the producer, the *Cahiers du Cinéma* critics gave far closer scrutiny to film form, finding hitherto overlooked recurring patterns and stratagems from which they could assert the director's world view. Crucially, it also involved looking at how the conditions of production impinged on them.

The English-speaking world was initially sceptical, but the success of the *nouvelle vague* (see page 86) helped to popularise the theory – dubbed 'auteurism' by the American critic Andrew Sarris – and, by the late 1960s, it had taken firm root. Ironically this was just when the French were moving to embrace structuralist theory, which turned the spotlight away from questions of authorship to focus on ideology and semiotics.

Auteurism survives in various forms, from the possessive credit 'A film by…' which has become obligatory for Hollywood directors (to the consternation of screenwriters), to DVD box sets, and innumerable critical studies. Today, critics and academics have largely dispensed with the polemical aspects that fired Truffaut et al, and balance an auteurist approach with a wider historical and anthropological perspective. For better, or more likely worse, it should also be noted that, with few exceptions, directors probably have less autonomy in Hollywood today than at any time since *Cahiers du Cinéma* elevated them to the status of author.

Frank Capra

One of the first directors to become a household name, Frank Capra bequeathed film lovers an adjective – 'Capra-esque' – and a noun: 'Capra-corn'. The former implies a brand of populist American idealism, while the latter denotes sentimental eyewash. Capra was capable of both (and not necessarily at the same time).

Born 1897, Bisacquino, Sicily
Importance Directed films that epitomised the 'American Dream'
Died 1991, La Quinta, California, United States

Capra's heyday runs from the early sound era through to the mid 1940s. He was at the height of his fame and fortune when he won the Academy Award for Best Director three times between 1935 and 1939. (He was also nominated in 1934, 1940 and 1947.) The achievement was particularly impressive, because Capra was under contract to Columbia Pictures, the smallest of the major studios in this period.

Capra started as a gag writer for Hal Roach and Mack Sennett. When Sennett's baby-faced star, Harry Langdon, switched to making features with First National, he took Capra with him, and promoted him to director on his second film, *The Strong Man* (1926). In 1928, Capra signed with Harry Cohn at Columbia, an association that immediately paid dividends in a string of vivacious popular comedies, notably slicker and quicker than most of their counterparts.

While Columbia lacked a large stable of big stars, Cohn was able to hire stars from other studios, and increasingly he entrusted them to Capra – most notably Clark Gable and Claudette Colbert for the bracingly cynical screwball smash *It Happened One Night* (1935), which swept the five top awards at the Oscars.

Nevertheless, Capra is remembered today not so much for his facility at comedy – or even, occasionally, darker fare like *The Bitter Tea of General Yen* (1933) – as for the impassioned Americanism he espoused in a series of preachy populist fables. Most often in collaboration with his favourite writer Robert Riskin, Capra responded to the Great Depression with optimistic New Deal parables like *American Madness* (1932), in which corrupt capitalists are redeemed by an honest banker (Walter Huston) who puts his faith in people, not collateral, or *Mr Deeds Goes to Town* (1936), when Gary Cooper's small-town poet resists the temptations that come his way with a large inheritance. *Mr Smith Goes to Washington* (1939) is a simplistic but nevertheless inspirational paean to integrity in a democracy prone to expediency, graft and compromise, and it gave James Stewart his first truly iconic role.

James Stewart plays George Bailey, a man on the edge of despair, in It's A Wonderful Life.

And then there is *It's A Wonderful Life* (1946), Capra's first film after the Second World War. A failure at the time, the film has since become more than a classic: it's a national institution. Although this spin on Dickens' *A Christmas Carol* is synonymous with homespun, small-town values, it achieves its emotional resonance precisely by stressing their limitations, even to the point of suicide. There is a darkness at the edges of even Capra's most whimsical films that comes through most strongly here – especially in the chilling 'unborn' sequence. Capra never had another hit.

Howard Hawks

A jack of all trades and the master of most, Howard Hawks directed more than 40 features between 1926 and 1970. They include westerns, gangster pictures, mystery thrillers, musicals, war films, comedies, action-adventure and even a sci-fi horror classic. For all this diversity, a Hawks film always bears the vivid imprint of his personality.

Born 1896, Goshen, Indiana, United States
Importance Prolific director of Hollywood films during the 'Golden Age'
Died 1977, Palm Springs, California, United States

Hawks is a crisp, self-effacing film-maker whose camera is almost always 'invisible' (the 'X' motif in *Scarface*, 1932, stands as the exception). Hawks considered himself an artisan, not an artist. He had a degree in engineering, and there is an engineer's pragmatic compulsion to streamline and recalibrate running through his pictures. Characters, lines of dialogue and entire scenes crop up with minor variations in films made decades apart, as if the perfect film was playing on a loop in his head. Only the faces have changed. It is no wonder he thrived in Hollywood's film factory.

He could be innovative. He did more than anyone to loosen up dialogue in the 1930s, encouraging his actors to cut each other off and to speed up their delivery. Someone timed Cary Grant and Rosalind Russell at 240 words a minute in the screwball classic *His Girl Friday* (1939). More importantly, he encouraged an attitude of play, establishing a rapport and mutual respect with his actors that brought out the best in stars like Grant, John Wayne, Humphrey Bogart and Lauren Bacall. Hawks enjoyed people, and it comes through.

A good part of his acuity was in going against the grain. At a time when films routinely telegraphed tragedy with crescendos of strings, Hawks' instinct was for stoicism and understatement – and for comedy. He was ahead of the game in the realisation that these modes

In Hawks' His Girl Friday, *the action of the film takes place in the space of just one day – mostly in the press room of a police station.*

were not mutually exclusive; that comic interplay can reveal character as well – or better – than a straight dramatic scene.

He made much of his experience as a pilot and palled around with Hemingway, but for all his mythomania, Hawks had little time for the clichés of the films' go-it-alone heroics – indeed he claimed that his masterpiece, *Rio Bravo* (1959), was inspired by his irritation over Gary Cooper's lone stand in Fred Zinnemann's *High Noon* (1952). No one in Hollywood was more keenly attuned to the alternating competitive and collaborative currents that run between men and women, or more invested in the integrity of the group – one reason *The Thing From Another World* (1951) is so horrific.

Preston Sturges

A blithe comic genius, Preston Sturges took the zany physical energy of the slapstick period and combined it with the sophisticated sexual banter of the screwball era to create some of the most inspired and entertaining films of the 1940s.

Born 1898, Chicago, Illinois, United States
Importance One of Hollywood's first writer-directors, and a master of dark humour
Died 1959, New York, New York, United States

Sturges' life story is as rich and strange as one of his madcap scenarios. His mother, Mary Desti, brought him up among the Riviera set. A self-styled bohemian, she was a friend of Isadora Duncan and Alistair Crowley. In his 20s, Sturges invented a kiss-proof lipstick at his mother's cosmetics firm, sold songs, then eloped with an heiress (Eleanor Post Hutton). On a whim he became a playwright. By the mid 1930s he was a successful screenwriter (*The Power and the Glory*; *Easy Living*) and, in 1940, he became one of the first writer-director-producers in Hollywood. He made seven smash hits in four years, anarchic comedies which rank amongst the funniest films ever made, but by 1950 his Hollywood career was over.

If Capra cherished an immigrant's ideal of America, Sturges offered a far more sardonic, knowing and worldly-wise perspective. His first film as writer-director, *The Great McGinty* (1940) is the story of a hobo whose gift for voter fraud eventually lands him a berth as the machine's reform candidate for mayor – a sweet deal he jeopardises when he falls in love and does the right thing for once. In *Sullivan's Travels* (1941) film-maker Joel McCrea bears the brunt of the ridicule for his earnest wish to represent 'the common man' when his true vocation is 'Ants in Your Pants 1937'. (Though Sturges slips in some genuine social conscience material on the sly.)

Sturges' heroes may be amiable innocents, like Capra's, but their naivety isn't necessarily a virtue. In *The Miracle of Morgan Creek*

(1944) Trudy Kockenlocker (Betty Hutton) does her bit for the boys going off to war and then some – after an excess of lemonade she wakes up married to someone she doesn't remember and definitively pregnant. It's an extraordinary film to come out of the home front at the height of the Second World War. *Hail the Conquering Hero* (1944) is even bolder, with Eddie Bracken masquerading as a war hero for his mum's sake, a harmless charade that spirals out of control when the whole town greets him at the station.

Sturges' relationship with Paramount soured. An attempt to mix slapstick with drama in the biopic *The Great Moment* (1944) didn't come off, and the decision to quit the studio and throw in his lot with Howard Hughes

Preston Sturges reputedly offered to sell his script for The Great McGinty *to Paramount for just $1 in order to be able to direct it in exchange.*

proved disastrous. Following a move to Twentieth Century Fox he delivered one last dark gem, *Unfaithfully Yours* (1948), a highbrow farce about a conductor whose murderous fantasies are scored to Rossini, Wagner and Tchaikovsky, but the film was too cruel for the popular audience. A comic western, *The Beautiful Blonde from Bashful Bend* (1949), was Sturges' first colour film and another flop. His era was over.

Otto Preminger

Drug addiction. Rape. Homosexuality. One of the first independent producer-directors, Otto Preminger tackled subjects that were considered taboo in American movies in the 1950s, and did so with a frankness that helped break the censorship codes of the time. By crediting screenwriter Dalton Trumbo on *Exodus* (1960) he also broke the blacklist.

Born 1906, Vienna, Austria
Importance One of the world's first independent producer-directors
Died 1986, New York, New York, United States

Preminger's battles with the Hollywood Production Code began in earnest with his first film as an independent producer, *The Moon is Blue* (1953), a sex comedy adapted from a play he had directed on Broadway in 1952. The authority refused to grant it a seal of approval, citing its 'unacceptably light attitude towards seduction, illicit sex, chastity and virginity'. None of this surprised Preminger, who had refused to dilute the script. He convinced United Artists to release the film anyway. It became a hit, exploiting the scandal, and undermining the censors and the studios that supported them.

Two years later, Preminger pulled the same trick with *The Man With the*

Although his reputation dwindled with erratic films in the 1970s, the 'New Hollywood' of the time owed more to Preminger than most other directors.

Golden Arm, the first American sound film to address drug addiction as a social problem and an illness. In between, he made the all-black musical *Carmen Jones* (1954). Preminger knew controversial material could sell tickets, but he was also a serious, thoughtful man who wanted to explore mature subjects: racism and the legal process (*Anatomy of a Murder*); Zionism (*Exodus*); Senate hearings (*Advise and Consent*); the Catholic Church (*The Cardinal*).

Cultured and sophisticated, not to mention arrogant and abrasive, Preminger was a Jewish émigré from Vienna, the son of the Austrian Attorney General. His first Hollywood efforts were undistinguished, and his career might have been over after a dispute with Darryl F Zanuck at Twentieth Century Fox. But he won kudos starring and directing in *Margin for Error* on Broadway, and was brought back to Fox to do the film version. Zanuck saw him as producer material, but allowed Preminger to take over directing duties on the thriller *Laura*, which turned out to be a hit. Half a dozen noirish suspense films followed, including *Fallen Angel* (1945), *Where the Sidewalk Ends* (1950) and *Angel Face* (1952).

Preminger's style isn't typical of noir. He minimises the expressionist subjectivity so fashionable at the time, preferring a more detached, 'objective' mise-en-scène, with unobtrusive, but often lengthy, takes and smooth, even tracking movements.

Good as the Fox films are, Preminger came into his own as an independent film-maker. The advent of CinemaScope allowed his supremely organised and realistic, but expansive, aesthetic to blossom. Preminger's work is sometimes called theatrical (in a positive sense), but it may be more appropriate to think of the courtroom as a model, with the spectator as juror, weighing the evidence of testimony and character as Preminger lays each aspect of the case before us.

BLACKLIST
The studios barred employment to actors, writers and directors who had fallen under suspicion of communist sympathies, or refused to testify during the House Un-American Activities Committee hearings of the late 1940s and 1950s. Victims included Abraham Polonsky, Joseph Losey and Dalton Trumbo.

THE STUDIO SYSTEM

It is easy to assert that film-making differs from other art forms in its prohibitive costs. But this is not entirely true. A director requires film, a camera and something to put in front of it. The costs of production are linked to expectations of box-office returns, and it is this business model that has dominated the art form: show business.

The first film-makers were independent entrepreneurs, inventors, photographers and amateur enthusiasts with the wherewithal to acquire a camera and film stock. As the public appetite for stories increased, productions became more elaborate and film technique more sophisticated. The films got longer. In 1894 the Lumière brothers' first films (or 'views') lasted less than a minute. By 1914, the Italian, Giovanni Pastrone, was recreating ancient Carthage with towering sets and a cast of thousands in his 180-minute adventure epic *Cabiria*. Such extravagance required significant investment and a physical stage large enough to accommodate it. It is no accident that the word 'studio' pertains to both a production company and the building in which films are shot.

By 1920, the US film industry had coalesced around Hollywood, California, with its sunny climate, varied topography and cheap labour costs. By the end of that decade eight studios were dominant: MGM, Paramount, Twentieth Century Fox, Warner Bros, United Artists, Universal, RKO and Columbia. (Disney did not start producing feature-length films until 1937.)

Although French, German and British film industries developed on broadly similar lines to Hollywood, American movies were popular across Europe from as early as the First World War (when indigenous film industries faltered). The exodus of home-grown talent as Nazism took hold in Germany, and the privations of the

Second World War consolidated Hollywood's position as the capital of film-making, at least in the Western World.

At the peak of their power in the 1930s and early 1940s, the Hollywood studios controlled production and distribution and enjoyed a significant stake in exhibition (they owned 3,000 of 18,000 cinemas in the US in 1945, including 70 per cent of the key first-run cinemas in the 92 largest American cities). Each with its own roster of stars, writers, directors and craftsmen under long-term contract, the studios (or 'majors') produced about 50 films a year throughout the 1930s. In this factory system it was rare for a writer, director or star to initiate a project, rather studio executives assigned material. The system encouraged genre film-making (see page 72), as studios sought a balanced slate of product, including musicals, comedies, westerns, dramas; prestigious 'A' movies and cheaper, shorter 'B' pictures.

> *'Hollywood has always been a cage ... a cage to catch our dreams.'*
>
> John Houston

The rapid turnover of product meant that any film most likely reflected a studio brand, rather than the artistic signature of any one creator. Metro-Goldwyn-Mayer (MGM), the wealthiest studio, was known for its glamour and its musicals. Warner Bros, one of the poorest, had a more proletarian, contemporary image, reflected in its contract stars James Cagney and Bette Davis.

Average weekly attendance reached a high of 80 million in 1930, before falling during the Depression. It rose again to 82 million in 1945 but declined rapidly and irreversibly with the arrival of television (down to 20 million in 1965). The same pattern was true in foreign markets.

The studio system declined rapidly. In 1946, the Supreme Court obliged them to dispose of their cinema holdings. Long-term contracts were no longer viable. Stars, directors and producers preferred to negotiate independent terms on a picture-by-picture basis. Most of the studio names endure, but now they are part of much larger conglomerates.

Billy Wilder

Master of the wisecrack, Billy Wilder brought a cynical temperament and a sharp, brittle wit to Hollywood dramas and comedies of the post-war era. *Double Indemnity* (1945) is archetypal noir, but Wilder is especially admired for his comedies.

Born 1906, Sucha, Austria-Hungary (now Poland)
Importance Post-war Hollywood director of both film noir and comedy
Died 2002, Los Angeles, California, United States

Wilder worked as a reporter in Vienna and a screenwriter in Berlin, where he collaborated with Fred Zinnemann, Robert and Curt Siodmak and Edgar G Ulmer on the lyrical city film *Menschen am Sonntag* (1930, *People on Sunday*). A Jew, he fled Hitler to Paris, then to the US.

He struck gold when Paramount teamed him with Charles Brackett to work on the Ernst Lubitsch screwball *Bluebeard's Eighth Wife* (1938). The two writers collaborated on 14 scripts in total, including films for Mitchell Leisen (*Midnight*, 1939) and Howard Hawks (*Ball of Fire*, 1941), but Lubitsch was his mentor. He claimed that he only became a director to protect his screenplays and, if the films' functional style tends to bear him out, it's also easy to understand how easily these dark, daring pictures might have been softened by a less abrasive personality at the helm.

The pessimism of film noir proved appealing to him, and *Double Indemnity* is one of the outstanding examples of the type, a bitter pill involving adultery, murder and greed orchestrated by Barbara Stanwyck's poisonous femme fatale. Although they're not strictly crime dramas, *The Lost Weekend* (1945), *Ace in the Hole* (1951) and *Sunset Blvd* (1950) all share a hard-boiled noir sensibility.

Wilder hit a creative peak in two collaborations with screenwriter I A L Diamond: *Some Like It Hot* and *The Apartment* (1960). The former was criticised at the time for tastelessness and vulgarity –

Internationally acclaimed as one of the greatest comedies ever made, Some Like It Hot *earned six Academy Award nominations when it was released.*

charges that could be levelled against many of his films, but which reflect Wilder's earthy and sardonic appreciation for the United States. Even so it was another box-office hit and earned six Academy Award nominations. He was back the next year to pick up the Best Picture award for *The Apartment*, a bitter pungent film, a comedy in name only, about 'the takers and the ones who get took'.

Wilder's attitude to women sometimes bordered on misogyny, but in these films he coaxed remarkably vulnerable, deeply sympathetic performances from Marilyn Monroe and Shirley MacLaine respectively. His men don't come off too badly, either. He made half a dozen films with Jack Lemmon (including *Irma la Douce*, 1963 and *Avanti*, 1972), finding in him an actor who could be selfish, cowardly, venal, and funny – all without alienating the audience.

Elia Kazan

Although his career was tarnished by his testimony before the House Un-American Activities Committee (HUAC) hearings, Kazan had a profound impact on American film and theatre. He directed Marlon Brando, James Dean and Montgomery Clift in movies that imprinted the psychological acting style known as 'The Method' on future generations.

Born 1909, Constantinople (now Istanbul), Turkey
Importance An early proponent of realism in film
Died 2003, New York, New York, United States

Kazan's family emigrated to the US from Anatolia when he was nine years old (*America, America* is based on his uncle's story). He went to the Yale Drama School on a scholarship, then into the Group Theatre under Lee Strasberg. There, he acted in productions of Clifford Odets' *Golden Boy* and *Waiting for Lefty*, flirted with Communism, and appeared in a few minor film roles in the early 1940s.

His early films are conventional but, in 1947, Kazan co-founded the Actors Studio, dedicated to the teachings of Stanislavsky, and he directed Brando in his Broadway debut, Tennessee Williams' *A Streetcar Named Desire*. The production was a sensation.

After America, America *– still his most under-appreciated film – Kazan turned to writing and made only three more pictures.*

Over the next two decades Kazan would be nominated for seven Tony awards and six Academy Awards. It is a period that coincides with the break-up of the studio-factory system, a shift towards location filming, greater realism, the beginning of the end of self-censorship and an explosion in psychological drama. Kazan was at the forefront of these changes, collaborating with playwrights Tennessee Williams, Arthur Miller and William Inge on Broadway and in Hollywood.

Kazan's 1951 film of *A Streetcar Named Desire* is primarily important as the permanent record of a landmark in American theatre – and the intense naturalism of Brando's breakthrough performance as Stanley Kowalski. Director and star collaborated twice more, on *Viva Zapata!* (1952) and *On the Waterfront* (1954), both high points in Brando's career. The latter was to remain Kazan's most revealing comment on his decision, in 1952, to name known Communists before the HUAC. In the film, Brando's longshoreman Terry Malloy testifies against his brothers (and his underworld brother) in the union, a choice for which he is badly beaten, but which is morally right and politically justified. Kazan's testimony, on the other hand, remains highly contentious, and allowed him to keep working while others were blacklisted (see page 35).

> **THE METHOD**
> The Method was based on the principles of the Russian theatre director Konstantin Stanislavsky, who stressed involved self-analysis and techniques like 'affective memory', which were designed to facilitate an actor's identification with his character.

East of Eden (1956) is an overwrought melodrama remembered for James Dean's first leading performance. *Baby Doll* (1956) was Tennessee Williams' only original screenplay, and another crack in the authority of the censors, and *A Face in the Crowd* (1957) is an astute satire about the political rise of folksy hobo Lonesome Rhodes (Andy Griffith). With each film you can see Kazan learning to trust the camera more, but it's really with *Wild River* (1960), *Splendor in the Grass* (1961) and *America, America* (1964) that he hits his peak, discovering an earthy sensuality and lyricism, and ultimately his own voice as a writer to tell the story of his uncle's terrible odyssey from Anatolia to the United States at the start of the twentieth century.

Nicholas Ray

A transitional figure in American film, Nicholas Ray came up in the late 1940s just as the studio system was beginning to break down. He brought psychological complexity, a febrile expressionism and existential angst to melodramas like *In a Lonely Place* (1950), *Johnny Guitar* (1954) and *Rebel Without a Cause* (1955). Yet Ray had burned out by 1963.

Born 1911, Galesville, Wisconsin, United States
Importance Exploited cynicism, melodrama and teen angst in making films of great intensity
Died 1979, New York, New York, United States

There is a heat and intensity to Ray's films that wasn't true of pre-war Hollywood. His debut, *They Live By Night* (1948), is a pastoral noir about Bonnie and Clyde-like fugitives, but Ray is more interested in the humanity, even the innocence of Farley Granger's young bank robber and his girlfriend Cathy O'Donnell, than in cops and robbers. Ray announces himself with a close-up of the lovers kissing, a romantic image broken by the voice of an off-screen narrator: 'This boy and this girl were never properly introduced to the world we live in.' They're the first in a long line of doomed outsiders who will make most of the running in Ray's films.

Ray was of the generation who felt the brunt of the Great Depression, and as a young man he was influenced by the leftwing politics of the Group Theatre crowd that also included Elia Kazan, Joseph Losey and the producer John Houseman. (Ray had also worked as an intern for the great modernist architect Frank Lloyd Wright.) Under contract to Howard Hughes at RKO, Ray credited the billionaire with protecting him from Communist witch-hunts. The price was a series of uninspired assignments that did little for his reputation or self-respect.

However, loaned out to Columbia for *In a Lonely Place*, he came up with an especially acrid Hollywood-on-Hollywood movie.

Humphrey Bogart played volatile screenwriter Dix Steele, a suspect in a murder case who falls in love with a neighbour, Laurel (Gloria Grahame). Again, the love story trumps the whodunit, but in this remarkably modern film the relationship breaks down into mistrust and hostility. Passionate and tender one minute, the couple are violent and fearful the next. (Ray and Grahame were on the point of divorce at the time.)

Ray came into his own in the 1950s, as if he felt compelled to give the lie to the conformity and prosperity of the times. He took the unease and alienation pulsing through post-war film noir and amplified it in baroque Freudian westerns like *Johnny Guitar*, cynical war pictures like *Bitter Victory* (1957), domestic melodramas and the quintessential teen-angst movie, *Rebel Without a Cause*.

Ray's romantic fatalism, coupled with acute visual intelligence and a taste for expressionist flourishes, made him a cause célèbre for the French auteurist critics at *Cahiers du Cinéma*. Yet for all his radical impulses, Ray failed to make the leap to independence. He left Hollywood to make the Samuel Bronston epics *King of Kings* (1961) and *55 Days in Peking* (1963) in Spain, but suffered a heart attack on the set of the latter, his days of alcohol and drug abuse catching up with him. He lived another 20 years, taught film, and dabbled on the margins, but outside the system he was as lost as his doomed heroes.

James Dean (right) with Ray on the set of Rebel Without a Cause. *The film defined Dean as a cultural icon.*

Orson Welles

A galvanizing force in American and European cinema, Orson Welles came to Hollywood in unique circumstances and threw away the rule book with his first film, *Citizen Kane* (1941). With his charismatic personality, technical virtuosity and storytelling verve, Welles embodied the idea of the film-maker as artist – and paid the price in years of exile.

Born 1915, Kenosha, Wisconsin, United States
Importance A maverick in the film-making industry, and a champion of innovative cinematography
Died 1985, Los Angeles, California, United States

Welles' key themes are power, megalomania, mortality and regret. He was a Shakespearean first, who came to film-making by way of the theatre. Between 1936 and 1938 he astonished the New York theatre scene with his radical interpretations of *Dr Faustus*, *Julius Caesar* and *Macbeth*. A radio production of H G Wells' *The War of the Worlds* performed in the style of a breaking-news bulletin terrified listeners across the country. When RKO proffered an invitation to Hollywood he was promised carte blanche, complete artistic freedom with the guarantee of final cut. He was 23 years old at the time.

Long held to be the greatest film ever made, *Citizen Kane* investigates the life of a brilliant entrepreneur and media tycoon from the perspectives of former colleagues and lovers. The film is remarkable for its sophisticated structure; its multifaceted portrait of a complex individual; and for the sheer range of aesthetic techniques it employs. Welles and cinematographer, Gregg Toland, restored to American film a heightened imaginative vision that had been dulled since the advent of sound. Their arsenal included deep-focus composition, dramatic low camera angles, expressionist lighting, dynamic travelling shots and numerous innovative transitions and montage sequences. *Citizen Kane* raised the bar for other film-makers, but Welles was not popular in the industry, and he made powerful enemies when he acknowledged similarities between Kane and the newspaper magnate William Randolph Hearst.

A regime change at RKO spelled the end of Welles' autonomy. His second feature, *The Magnificent Ambersons* (1942), was drastically re-cut by the studio while Welles was shooting the Pan-American propaganda film *It's All True* in Brazil, which was ultimately abandoned. Almost all of Welles' subsequent American films would suffer from studio-imposed cuts, and many of the independent projects he embarked on in Europe would languish as he diverted his energies elsewhere, in search of financing or new ideas.

Even so, the myth of Welles the underachiever who, in his own words, 'started at the top and have been working my way down ever since', needs to be offset against the substantial achievements of

Citizen Kane is often cited as one of the most innovative works in the history of film.

the later years, including the film noir *Touch of Evil* (1958), the melancholy Shakespeare adaptation *Chimes at Midnight* (1965), and his witty essay on art and forgery, *F For Fake* (1974).

Maya Deren

Inspired by the early films of Jean Cocteau and Luis Buñuel, Maya Deren was at the forefront of the American experimental film movement. Her films and writings and, equally importantly, her efforts to establish an independent network to exhibit and support non-narrative film, laid the groundwork for the American avant-garde that took root in the 1950s.

Born 1917, Kiev, Ukraine
Importance A forerunner of the American avant-garde movement in film
Died 1961, New York, New York, United States

Born Eleanora Derenkowsky, Deren grew up in Syracuse, New York after her family fled anti-Semitism in the Ukraine. She studied journalism and political science, then got a masters in English Literature and symbolist poetry in 1939. She was an assistant to the dancer and choreographer Katherine Dunham until 1943, when she adopted the name 'Maya', married the Czech cameraman Alexander Hammid and switched her focus to film.

Meshes of the Afternoon (1943) is credited to both Deren and Hammid. This 14-minute film uses surrealist imagery (a flower, a key, a knife, various doppelgangers, and a mysterious robed figure with a mirror face); discontinuous editing; slow motion; super-imposition; and a cyclical structure to convey a dream or trance state. Deren appears as a woman in a suburban hacienda setting (identified, ironically, as Hollywood), and Hammid also has a small role as a man who wakes her from sleep, but any attempt to read the film as a conventional narrative is disrupted by its disorientating editing strategies. Nevertheless, we can see that the film expresses anxiety about a woman's fragmented sense of her self in relation to an illusory yet constrictive domestic space.

Meshes of the Afternoon draws on the European tradition of surrealist film that had largely petered out after the silent era (in 1943,

Meshes of the Afternoon *was selected for preservation in the United States National Film Registry by the Library of Congress in 1990.*

Deren also collaborated on a film with Marcel Duchamp, *Witches Cradle*, though it was never completed). In her subsequent films (none longer than 18 minutes) Deren is more interested in looking at the sensual, dynamic female form in a spatial, non-linear environment, often counterpointing social space with natural landscapes. Dance is another significant element in these films: *At Land* (1944); *A Study in Choreography for Camera* (1945); *Ritual and Transfigured Time* (1946); *Meditation on Violence* (1948). In 1947, Deren travelled to Haiti for eight months, where she became fascinated with Voodoo rituals and beliefs, the subject of her classic 1953 ethnographic text *Divine Horsemen*.

As with other experimental film-makers, Maya Deren's contribution to the development of cinema is routinely marginalised, but her influence extends beyond the next generation of American avant-garde film-makers to contemporary directors like David Lynch and Claire Denis.

WOMEN IN FILM

Film-making has always been dominated by men. However, a handful of remarkable women have also blazed a trail. Even so, despite the situation improving in recent years, in 2006, the Directors Guild of America reported that only 13 per cent of its members were women.

When the statistics include cinematographers, editors, writers and production editors, the numbers are not much better: just 17 per cent of these positions were filled by women in the top 250 grossing films of 2005.

Actresses have fought to close the pay gap over the years, but only a few have mustered real power, and the autonomy and independence of the women they have played has fluctuated wildly. Feminist critics point to the 1940s and to the 1970s as relatively progressive eras for the representation of women on screen.

Frenchwoman Alice Guy was the head of production at Gaumont from 1897 to 1906, and directed her first film, *The Life of Christ*, in 1906. An innovator, Guy experimented with colour, special effects and synchronous sound decades before these things became the industry norm. Guy moved to the United States in 1907, and directed several more films before returning to France in 1922.

Lois Weber was the most prominent woman director of the silent period. A writer and actress, Weber was an evangelist who addressed social issues like birth control, capital punishment and abortion in controversial but moralistic films like *The Hypocrites* (1915) and *Where are My Children*

'I'm not interested in seeing a film just made by a woman – not unless she is looking for new images.'

Agnes Varda

(1916). Weber's fortunes declined in the 1920s after her divorce from collaborator, Phillips Smalley, and her one 'talkie', *White Heat* (1934) was not well received.

A screenwriter and editor, Dorothy Arzner persuaded Paramount to let her direct *Fashions for Women* in 1927, and went on to make a dozen more 'women's pictures' over the next five years. She went independent in 1932, and made some of her best-known films with stars like Katharine Hepburn, Rosalind Russell, Maureen O'Hara and Lucille Ball. Arzner later disclaimed any feminist intent on her part, but that hasn't stopped critics from finding subversive ideological elements in her work.

Arzner made her last feature in 1943. Six years later, the actress Ida Lupino was the next woman to pick up the megaphone, helming half a dozen low-budget films between 1949 and 1954. Lupino's economical, crisp B movies include 1950's *Outrage* (about rape), and *The Bigamist* (1955). She subsequently directed more than 100 episodes for television.

In Europe, Leni Riefenstahl was a talented film-maker who dedicated herself to propaganda for the Nazi party. The situation improved in the latter half of the twentieth century with greater awareness of feminism and more fragmented, independent and public-subsidized film production. In France, Agnes Varda has a strong claim to the first new-wave film, *La Pointe Courte* (1954). Fifty years later, Varda is still making films. Marguerite Duras, Chantal Ackerman, Claire Denis, Catherine Breillat and others have built up an impressive and multifaceted French feminist cinema.

Internationally, their sisters include the New Zealander Jane Campion; the Indian Mira Nair; Iranian Samira Makhmalbaf; Hong Kong's Ann Hui; Canadian Deepa Mehta; and British Lynne Ramsey, Sally Potter and Andrea Arnold. In 2004, Sofia Coppola became the first American woman to be nominated for the Academy Award for Best Director.

Stanley Kubrick

A rationalist with a profound curiosity about the human psyche, Stanley Kubrick oversaw his characters' often self-destructive pursuits with dispassionate reserve. He took the long view on human evolution and social conditioning, finding little hope for individual free will. Nevertheless there are consolations in the invention and beauty of Kubrick's art, in his humour and intelligence.

Born 1928, New York, New York, United States
Importance Controversial director with a portfolio of cerebral and thought-provoking films
Died 1999, Hertfordshire, England

In an industry traditionally sceptical of artists, Kubrick was virtually unique in securing the long-lasting patronage of a major studio – Warner Bros – who allowed him complete autonomy to make his own films at his own pace. A legendary perfectionist who regularly shot dozens – sometimes hundreds – of takes, Kubrick repaid them with prestigious films that were cerebral and provocative.

Kubrick was often portrayed as a recluse in the press, but this is largely a myth and may have resulted from his aversion to air travel.

A professional photojournalist in his teens, Kubrick made a couple of unremarkable documentary shorts in the early 1950s, then financed two noir thrillers independently: *Fear and Desire* (1953) and *Killer's Kiss* (1955). *Paths of Glory* (1957) was his first picture with a big star – Kirk Douglas – and remains a trenchant anti-war film. But director and star-producer fell out on the Roman epic *Spartacus* (1960), his only film-for-hire. Kubrick gravitated to 'difficult' subject matter: a risky film of Nabokov's controversial novel *Lolita* (1962), about an intellectual who takes a 14-year-old girl as his lover. In *Dr Strangelove, or: How I Learned to Stop Worrying and Love the Bomb* (1964) he tackled the nightmare of Mutually Assured Destruction as inspired black comedy.

2001: A Space Odyssey (1968) redefined the sci-fi genre. With its radical structure (a single cut elides four million years), scant dialogue and oblique narrative, this was the first film to emulate the philosophical seriousness of writers like Clarke and Philip K Dick, and the first to see that special effects could become an integral component in the art form. The film combines a typically cold Kubrickian rationalism with a genuine sense of awe, mystery and beauty. In this film and the ones that followed – a highly controversial stab at Anthony Burgess's novel *A Clockwork Orange* (1971); the seventeenth-century picaresque *Barry Lyndon* (1975); Stephen King's horror *The Shining* (1980) – Kubrick sought to transcend prefabricated genre models, taking audacious leaps with narrative structure and making emphatic aesthetic choices (slow zooms and natural light in *Barry Lyndon*; creepy tracking shots in *The Shining*).

As the gaps between his pictures grew longer Kubrick's instincts dulled somewhat. Neither the Vietnam War film *Full Metal Jacket* (1987) nor the elegant sexual daydream *Eyes Wide Shut* (1999) registered with the old force, though each offers further proof of his intellectual ambition and technical brilliance.

The Renegade

John Cassavetes

John Cassavetes rewrote the rules of engagement. Rejecting Hollywood's production methods and the industrial grammar that made studio films safe and predictable, Cassavetes hit on an alternative process that was more emotionally volatile and raw. He wrote and directed a dozen turbulent, truthful films and inspired subsequent generations of film-makers.

Born 1929, New York, New York, United States
Importance Godfather of American Independent Film
Died 1989, Los Angeles, California, United States

A successful young television actor, Cassavetes embarked on *Shadows* in 1956, an 'improvised' film financed through private (and public) donors. Performed by students in the acting class Cassavetes taught, who also doubled as the crew on borrowed equipment, the film was shot quickly, then revised in scripted reshoots. It was 1958 before Cassavetes signed off on the edit. To his surprise, it won a Venice Film Festival prize and excellent reviews in Europe, which led to a directing contract with Paramount.

If *Shadows* has since become a milestone in the history of independent film, Cassavetes' fourth film, *Faces* (1968) is both a greater accomplishment and an

Cassavetes regularly turned his films around in the editing to more ambiguous, often aggravating, effect.

important turning point, allowing him to assert his independence. Largely shot in his own home, using a cast and crew of actor friends and collaborators from *Shadows*, *Faces* is a sour, intentionally unfunny comedy about the breakdown of an upper-middle-class marriage.

In this, and his subsequent films, Cassavetes exposed audiences to a more intense and challenging emotional pitch than they were accustomed to. The films were scripted, but shot in a manner that allowed the actors greater freedom of movement – he shot almost everything in long master takes, and his cameramen were expected to follow the actors' lead, in a manner reminiscent of *cinéma vérité*. Lighting, sound and continuity were all sacrificed to a greater spontaneity. By inviting imperfection into the frame he hit on a new, vital and authentic pulse. The rhythm is different, too. Mistrustful of fixed ideas or anything that smacked of resolution, Cassavetes embraced hesitations, repetitions and *longeurs* as tools of disruption and misdirection.

> **CINÉMA VÉRITÉ**
> A term used generally to denote a you-are-there style of coverage in which a hand-held camera is the tacit acknowledgement of the crew's presence or communicates a sense of immediacy and reality.

Cassavetes' uncompromising approach kept him on the margins of the mainstream, although his career as an actor (*The Dirty Dozen*; *Rosemary's Baby*) helped pay for his own pictures. *Faces* and *A Woman Under the Influence* (which he distributed himself) were successful though, and even received Academy Award nominations. As film production became more expensive, Cassavetes was forced to capitulate to the mainstream with the feminist thriller *Gloria* (1980), for which his wife, Gena Rowlands, won an Oscar nomination.

Cassavetes died from cirrhosis of the liver at 59, but not before he completed the crazy, heartfelt, haunting dream-movie, *Love Streams*

'In my opinion, these people and these small emotions are the greatest political force there is.'

(1984). Like all his films, it was charged with the joys and pangs of emotional expression.

Robert Altman

Robert Altman was the oldest, the thorniest and most irascible of the great 'Hollywood Renaissance' directors of the 1970s. For Altman, the studio was the enemy, and many of his most interesting pictures were sly critiques on traditional film genres.

Born 1925, Kansas City, Kansas, United States
Importance An enemy of the studio film, who satirised many traditional film genres
Died 2006, Los Angeles, California, United States

A late bloomer, Altman worked in television for nearly 20 years. His greatest success, *MASH* (1970), was only his third feature. This comedy about a military field hospital was set in the Korean War but Altman fudged the specifics so that it was understood to be about Vietnam. Twentieth Century Fox expected a conventional comedy, but Altman was able to fly under the radar and create what was surely the most anarchic, anti-authoritarian, anti-military, anti-religious film to have come out of Hollywood until then.

In Altman's free-form, improvisational method everything was up for grabs. This was the first of the large ensemble pieces he covered fly-on-the-wall style, eavesdropping on conversations almost at random (all the actors had microphones and were instructed to stay in character), leaning heavily on the zoom lens. It was a jazzy, open-ended mode of film-making he would return to often.

MASH struck a chord with the counterculture and established Altman as an important talent. He responded with a combination of oddball comic allegories, European-influenced art films and revisionist genre pictures, but it would be decades before he enjoyed such popular acclaim again.

Nashville (1975) was a major statement, lobbed like a stink bomb

'When I'm making a film I'm not making propaganda, I try to show things the way I see they are.'

As a film-maker, Altman was a behaviourist – fascinated by interaction, less interested in story.

into the hoopla of the nation's bicentennial celebrations. Altman imagines a grassroots presidential campaign cultivating the country and western constituency – thus supplying a focal point to his satiric panorama. It's a film of party pieces and exuberant acting out, but whether Altman is jeering or cheering is not always easy to determine.

His brand of unruly satire proved very erratic and his stock in the industry was equally up and down. After the failure of the musical *Popeye* (1980) he was forced to work on a smaller scale over the next ten years, producing several fine chamber pieces. He bounced back with the jaundiced Hollywood-insider comedy *The Player* (1992) and another LA epic, *Short Cuts* (1993), based on the stories of Raymond Carver. The country house mystery *Gosford Park* (2001) and his final film, *A Prairie Home Companion* (2006), were further variations of the multi-strand structure to which he kept returning.

Altman's body of work amounts to a teeming, caustic and compassionate human comedy; a singularly astringent, often cynical, view of America and Americana; and a rowdy celebration of the same.

The Perfectionist

Carl Dreyer

Caricatured as a forbidding, austere Scandinavian, Carl Theodor Dreyer was unquestionably committed and serious in his pursuit of inner reality, but his intensity and originality make for spellbinding cinema. Dreyer simply scrutinized humanity more closely than any other director of his time.

Born 1889, Copenhagen, Denmark
Importance A director with remarkable insight into the human psyche
Died 1968, Copenhagen, Denmark

Dreyer's mother, a maid, had her child out of wedlock and put him up for adoption – dying 18 months later, after attempting a self-induced abortion. He reportedly revered his dead mother and despised his foster parents. Coincidentally or not, Dreyer's best-known films repeatedly turn to the suffering of women, including the martyred St Joan of Arc and the persecuted pastor's wife in *Day of Wrath* (1943). Dreyer's career is strangely weighted. He was 30 when he first directed (after working as a journalist and screenwriter); he made nine features between 1919 and 1930, in Norway, Germany and France, including *The Parson's Widow* (1920); a gay psychological drama, *Michael* (1924); and *Master of the House* (1925). Despite their critical reputation, neither *The Passion of Joan of Arc* (1928) nor *Vampyr* (1932) met with commercial success, and Dreyer suffered a nervous breakdown shortly afterwards. He made only five more features over the next three

The Passion of Joan of Arc *(1928) was based on the actual trial transcripts.*

decades, one of which (*Two People*, 1945) was suppressed at his own request. These were interspersed with public information films made for the Danish government.

Part of the reason for the large gaps between his later projects is that Dreyer was rigorous and often radical in his attention to aesthetics: the quality of the light; the composition of the frame; the artfully modulated rhythms of movement and cutting; and above all the depth of the performances. Shot over an 18-month period, *The Passion of Joan of Arc* is a film made overwhelmingly of close-ups, a unique and disorientating strategy that mirrors the anguish and bewilderment of the maid of Orleans.

Vampyr is an extraordinary contribution to the cinema of the fantastic, a horror film that derives its uncanny power from an eerie half-light, as if it had been shot somewhere between the real world and the surreal (Dreyer called it 'a waking dream'). And the seventeenth-century witch-hunt drama *Day of Wrath* (1943) – filmed under Nazi occupation – developed the director's penchant for lengthy, gliding pans, and adopted a slow, hypnotic pace – yet the film is also surprisingly sensual and disturbing.

Ordet (1955) goes further still. Set largely within the farmhouse of the Borgen family, this is a chamber piece about faith. Morten, the patriarch, is a devout Christian, but two of his three grown sons are agnostic at best; the third, Johannes, studied theology but came home convinced that he is Jesus Christ. It remains an open question whether Johannes is deluded or truly touched by God. Dreyer's graceful, patient direction allows this increasingly intense parable to live and breathe; it is simultaneously a very natural and a highly stylised piece. By the end, for many, it becomes an unforgettable and transcendent experience.

Gertrud (1964), Dreyer's last film, was rejected everywhere for its supposedly uncinematic procession of duologues and long, long takes. Yet this study of a determined, independent woman who abandons her husband and rejects a series of suitors over the years now seems ahead of its time, a characteristically uncompromising, heartfelt and supremely refined meditation on the human soul.

Jean Renoir

**The most cherished of French film-makers at home and
abroad, Jean Renoir made a string of masterpieces in the
1930s, including *La Grande Illusion* (1937) and *La Règle du Jeu*
(*The Rules of the Game*, 1939). These lucid, fluid
and open films engage with reality in a direct
manner that made a lasting impression on the
post-war generation of film-makers and critics.**

Born 1894, Paris, France
Importance France's
most feted film-maker
Died 1979, Los Angeles,
California, United States

The son of the artist, Pierre-Auguste Renoir, Jean made
his first and last films in the bucolic estate in the
Auvergne where he grew up. His wife, Catherine Hessling, had been
his father's model, and she starred in Jean's first films: *La Fille de l'eau*
(1925) and *Nana* (1926). He also dabbled in a couple of experimental
shorts. He really seems to have found himself as film-maker with the
arrival of synchronous sound recording, with its promise of putting
real life on screen in all its voluble confusion.

Although he worked across many genres, from anarchic comedies
like *Boudu Sauvé des Eaux* (*Boudu Saved from Drowning*, 1932) through
crime, romance and historical
epics, Renoir quickly developed
his own signature style: a
preference for location shooting,
lengthy and mobile (though
generally unobtrusive) takes, and
deep compositions allowing for

*'A director makes only one
movie in his life. Then he
breaks it into pieces and
makes it again.'*

plenty of movement within the frame. According to his first and most
ardent champion, *Cahiers du Cinéma* founder André Bazin, this
aesthetic reflected Renoir's 'faith in the real world' (as opposed to faith
in the image). Renoir himself felt that it liberated the actors, allowing
for more spontaneity and spatial continuity.

Contemporary critics were dubious about such techniques, which came across as raw and unrefined, and the crazy cross-currents of comedy and drama that went with them. His 1930s' films were plugged into the leftwing popular-front politics of those tumultuous times – most explicitly the tragi-comedy *Le Crime de Monsieur Lange* (1936) – and the case can be made that his shooting style was inherently egalitarian.

The First World War prison-escape film *La Grande Illusion* was hailed as a powerful pacifist statement, but it's really about class barriers. Just a year later, the country-house farce *La Règle du Jeu* scandalised the public with its level-headed look

Jean Renoir and Julien Carette in The Rules of the Game. *Banned following its release, the film has since been heralded as one of the best of all time.*

at giddy lovers and charlatans on the eve of war, 'dancing on the precipice of a volcano', as Renoir put it. After the premiere nearly induced a riot, the distributor ordered 13 minutes of cuts, and it was subsequently banned in France for being too demoralising. Only when a full-length cut was restored in the late 1950s did the film assume its mantle as one of the greatest ever made, an evaluation that now seems unassailable.

Renoir fled Paris the day before the Germans came in, and spent the next decade working within the Hollywood system. The American films are not negligible but minor. His late period really blossomed after he left, first for India (*The River*, 1951) then home to France for a trio of rich, sensual, theatrical comedies.

ANIMATION

Although it has often been dismissed as 'kids' stuff', the animated film – or cartoon – may be the purest and most free form of film-making. Animation has a history stretching back to the first decade of the twentieth century, and among its multifaceted masterpieces are films from North America, Eastern Europe, Great Britain and Japan.

In the West, throughout the second half of the twentieth century, the films of Walt Disney played a part in almost every childhood. The most commercially successful of all animators, Disney had relentless drive and determination combined with an intuitive, empathetic sense of storytelling and character. From the first, his *Silly Symphony* cartoons found their heart and humour in cutely caricatured, anthropomorphised animals in realistically etched settings. Mickey Mouse, originally known as Mortimer, made his debut in 1928.

Disney wasn't the first, however. He was influenced by Windsor McCay, a lightning-sketch artist who toured with his whimsical heroine Gertie the Dinosaur from 1914, to the amazement and delight of audiences. With his superb draughtsmanship and playful sense of mischief, McCay outlined the direction the American cartoon would take over the next three decades, anticipating not only the Disney shorts but the anarchic Looney Tunes school at Warner Bros: Termite Terrace.

Meanwhile in Russia, Ladislaw Starewich used stop-motion to bring three-dimensional sculptures of insects to life and, like McCay, he introduced an element of self-reflexivity in his films, evident as early as *The Cameraman's Revenge* (1912). A decade later, in Germany, Lotte Reiniger pioneered another form of stop-motion, silhouette animation, in the elegant, gorgeously colour-tinted and feature-length *The Adventures of Prince Achmed* (1926). Disney, too, embraced colour at an early stage, when live-action films were overwhelmingly in black and white. He embarked on his first feature in 1937. *Snow White and the Seven Dwarfs* almost bankrupted his fledgling studio, but it proved the blockbuster hit of its day. Like subsequent Disney animated features, it was a traditional European fairytale prettied up; its traumas come sugarcoated. Disney made one bold art film, *Fantasia* (1940). Its failure with critics and the public convinced him to stick to bedtime stories thereafter.

The quality of the Disney studio's output declined over time, and especially after Walt's death in 1966. By the late 1980s, animated features seemed locked in terminal decline. Instead, however, we've seen a period of intense excitement and innovation.

Japanese anime films, ranging from Miyazaki Hayao's enchanting fairytales to hard-edged contemporary fantasies like *Akira* (1988), have earned an enthusiastic cult following in the West. Satirical, and sometimes surreal, television shows like *South Park* and *The Simpsons* have cultivated an adult audience. And Nick Park has delighted young and old with his very British, very quirky 'claymation' comedies featuring Wallace and Gromit.

We've had animated art films including Richard Linklater's rotoscoped *Waking Life* (2001) and *A Scanner Darkly* (2006); Marjane Satrapi's autobiographical *Persepolis* (2007), based on her graphic novel; and Ari Folman's *Waltz with Bashir* (2008), exploring his suppressed memories of military service in Lebanon. On top of all this, the Pixar studio has galvanised the industry with its unbroken run of computer-animated hits from *Toy Story* (1995) to *WALL-E* (2008).

'Animation can explain whatever the mind of man can conceive. This facility makes it the most versatile and explicit means of communication yet devised for quick mass appreciation.'

Walt Disney

Kenji Mizoguchi

Arguably Japan's greatest film-maker, Kenji Mizoguchi is best remembered for half a dozen exquisite, harrowing historical melodramas made in the 1950s. In these films Mizoguchi refined a style based on long, flowing sequence shots and a detached, yet tragic, sensibility often centred on the plight of women in society.

Born 1898, Tokyo, Japan
Importance The quintessential Japanese film-maker and master of the single shot
Died 1956, Kyoto, Japan

The roots of Mizoguchi's art may lie in his childhood. The family was impoverished when he was seven, and his 14-year-old sister Suzu was put up for adoption and then sold to a geisha house. It was through Suzu's efforts that Kenji was able to study art and become a painter, and later direct films. Mizoguchi began his career in the silent era, although the earliest surviving print is *The Water Magician* (*Taki No Shiraito*, 1933), by which time he had made more than 60 films of all types.

Mizoguchi was a pictorialist and a perfectionist, who regularly demanded as many as 30 takes before he was satisfied. By the time of *The Water Magician*, he was well on the way to developing his primary cinematic mode, which was to convey each scene in a single, unbroken shot. Mizoguchi's camera is rarely static; slow, graceful pans and crane shots make note of artful details in the decor or environment, so that each sequence takes on a harmonious atmosphere or poetic colouring. In Japan, this style has been linked to classical Noh theatre and to the picture scroll, *emakimono*, and Mizoguchi may be considered the most quintessentially Japanese of film-makers. Yet he was not merely

'Mizoguchi alone inspires the feeling of a specific language and universe that have no one to answer to except themselves and himself.'

Jacques Rivette

a traditionalist; his films do not shy away from implicating repressive power structures, gender relationships and economic exploitation.

1936 was a breakthrough year: *Osaka Elegy* and *Sisters of the Gion* focused on the hard choices faced by women in contemporary Japan. Mizoguchi followed these with what may be his first masterpiece, *Story of the Late Chrysanthemums* (1939), a tragic tale about a nineteenth-century kabuki actor and the sacrifices his lover, a servant, makes for him.

Mizoguchi came into his own in the 1950s. He won prizes at the Venice Film Festival three years straight, with *The Life of Oharu* (1952), about the decline of a courtier to prostitution; the ghost story *Ugetsu Monogatari* (1953); and *Sansho the Bailiff* (1954), about two children stolen from their mother and sold into slavery. These, plus *Chikamatsu Monogatari* (*The Crucified Lovers,* 1954) and *Street of Shame* (1956) constitute the core Mizoguchi titles.

By this point Mizoguchi was able to select his own material and his key collaborators (cameraman Kazuo Miyagawa; writer Yoshikata

Set in sixteenth-century Japan, and starring Masayuki Mori and Machiko Kyŷ, Ugetsu Monogatari *is credited as Mizoguchi's finest film.*

Yoda). The eloquence of Miyagawa's crane movements, the refinement of gesture Mizoguchi demanded of his actors, and the finely balanced compassion and detachment that is his trademark, have resulted in some of the most indelible and sublime moments in all film.

Luis Buñuel

Film's foremost surrealist, Luis Buñuel relished the comedy of human desire and its infinite frustrations. He exposed hypocrisy, made a mockery of clerics, puritans, authoritarians, the privileged and the complacent and, over time, refined a subtle, elegant mise-en-scène (see page 11) that made him a favourite of the same bourgeoisie he loved to excoriate.

Born 1900, Calanda, Spain
Importance A critical satirist of the bourgeoisie
Died 1983, Mexico City, Mexico

A man stands behind a woman, brandishes a razor, and then calmly slices open her eyeball. These were the shocking first images Buñuel committed to celluloid (he also played the man). The film was *Un Chien Andalou* (1929), a short co-directed with Buñuel's college friend and compatriot, Salvador Dalí, based on the principle that nothing in its succession of dream images should be reducible to rational explanation. Nevertheless, there is an unmistakable subversive charge to its incongruities.

The Spaniards collaborated a second time the following year, on *L'âge d'or* although Dalí soon left the project. This time Buñuel's anticlericalism and eroticism ran rampant – the film concludes by linking Jesus Christ with an orgy. The film scandalised Paris, sparking riots and threats of excommunication against the film's backer. It was promptly banned (and remained that way for three decades).

With Spain falling into civil war Buñuel quit Europe, first for the US, then emerging in the late

'Motion pictures act directly upon the spectator… Because of this the cinema is capable of stirring the spectator as perhaps no other art. But as no other art can, it is also capable of stupefying him.'

Buñuel was well known for his atheism. During a 1960 interview, he famously declared, 'I am still, thank God, an atheist'.

1940s in Mexico. For all that he was working within a commercial industry, Buñuel did extraordinary work there, ranging from the neo-realist *Los Olvidados* (1950), about Mexico City slum kids, to comic thriller *The Criminal Life of Archibaldo de la Cruz* (1955).

In 1960, his prestige was such that he was invited back to make a film in Spain. He made *Viridiana*, one of his most biting satires, a scathing portrait of a 'respectable' landowner who lusts after his niece, a pious young nun. The Franco regime disowned the film but it won the Palme d'Or at Cannes and set Buñuel on course for the third and final phase of his career, as an international art-house director. It was in this period, 1960 to 1977, that he made his most famous films, including *The Exterminating Angel* (1962); *Diary of a Chambermaid* (1964); *Belle de Jour* (1967); *The Discreet Charm of the Bourgeoisie* (1972), which won an Oscar; and *That Obscure Object of Desire* (1977).

Max Ophüls

'For me, life is movement', declares Lola Montes in the 1955 film of that name. The same might be said of Max Ophüls, whose proto-feminist films vibrate with the life of the camera in motion, tracking and dollying in an impeccably graceful dance with his players. No matter where Ophüls was, his melodramas exude exquisite sophistication, elegance and grace, while revealing romantic infatuation, sexual desire and heartbreak.

Born 1902, Saarland, Germany
Importance Accomplished studio film-maker and master of sequence shots
Died 1957, Hamburg, Germany

Born Max Oppenheimer, Ophüls was a musician, an actor and a theatre director before working his way up at the UFA (Universum Film AG) studios in Germany. His first great film is *Liebelei* (1933) a tragic love story based on a play by Arthur Schnitzler. When the Nazis came to power, Ophüls fled to France, though he also worked further afield. *La Signora di Tutti* (1934) has an experimental flashback structure and rehearses the elaborate tracking shots that the director would refine over time.

It was some time before Ophüls established himself in Hollywood. *The Exile* (1947) was a swashbuckler with Douglas Fairbanks Jr. He was hired, then promptly fired, by Howard Hughes on the ill-fated *Vendetta*. But *Letter from an Unknown Woman* (1948), and the film noirs *Caught* (1949) and *The Reckless Moment* (1949) are among the finest studio films of the period. The first, especially, carves an indelible, overwhelmingly tragic impression of a hopeless passion from an apparently trite story about a woman (Joan Fontaine) seduced and abandoned by a concert pianist (Louis Jourdan).

Returning to Europe, Ophüls made four more films in which his florid style reached sublime heights. *La Ronde* (1950), from Schnitzler again, is the most famous, a droll but delicate comedy in which a series of lovers come together and part ways under the cynical, indulgent eye of Anton Walbrook's master of ceremonies. Then (after *Le Plaisir*) there is *Madame de…* (1953), which has a similar merry-go-round structure, following a pair of earrings exchanged between lovers. This dazzling conceit betokens the director's fascination with surface detail, a fascination that, on closer examination, reveals tremendous depths of feeling. And finally we come back to *Lola Montès*, Ophüls' most baroque, trenchant and self-reflexive artifice, with Martine Carol as a notorious nineteenth-century courtesan now reduced to replaying her amorous adventures in the circus.

Ophüls' ornate and flowing visuals were once dismissed as 'decorative'; his abiding empathy for forlorn and exploited women, 'old-fashioned'. But his style is not an affectation – indeed its grace and sensitivity are often ascribed as feminine attributes.

The sequence shots that are his signature tell myriad stories; they are orchestrated in tandem with the actors' movements precisely to illuminate the characters' thoughts and feelings. Each shot immerses us into a world, and modulates our sympathies as we shift from one lover's perspective, to another's.

Ophül's work is known for his tracking shots and elaborate camera movements.

Yasujiro Ozu

Yasujiro Ozu is a special case, a film-maker who developed a unique, highly idiosyncratic style, returned repeatedly to the same handful of mundane domestic themes – which he treated with unfailing understatement – yet was able to work with minimal commercial compromise for more than 40 years. His work is exotic and universal, simple and profound.

Born 1903, Tokyo, Japan
Importance A paragon of Japanese film-making
Died 1963, Tokyo, Japan

The mature Ozu style is immediately identifiable. He favoured a fixed camera position, usually about a metre off the ground (partly because his characters are most often sitting on tatami mats). He rarely used anything but a 50mm lens, and largely avoided panning or zooms. Dialogue scenes are cut so that the camera is always on the

speaker. He 'crosses' the notional 180-degree line with impunity. Interior scenes are interspersed with a distinctive variation on the standard establishing shot, which, in Ozu's hands, becomes a montage of three or four exterior urban landscapes, denoting not only geography but, more importantly, the passage of time.

Furthermore, almost all the late Ozu films are *shomingeki*,

Ozu's art as a film-maker is a process of contemplation, modulation and refinement.

contemporary, domestic dramas about typical middle-class families. Several of them hinge on the relationship between aging parents and grown children (especially daughters) on the verge of marriage and leaving home. (Ozu himself was a bachelor who lived with his mother until she died, just three months before he passed away.)

These are films about family relationships, and mix social comedy with a poignant appreciation that the wheel is turning, and solitude awaits. These themes are as characteristic as Ozu's shooting style and his small stock company of favourite actors. The films even have similar (English) titles: *Early Summer* (1951); *Early Spring* (1953); *Late Autumn* (1960); *The End of Summer* (1961); *An Autumn Afternoon* (1962).

His films are beautifully structured, but 'story' is so far in the background it is almost non-existent. Ozu is more interested in moods and tone, nuance and flavour – a bittersweet blend that mixes melancholy, regret, irony, affection and good humour, regularly chased down with copious amounts of sake.

His most celebrated film is *Tokyo Story* (*Tokyo Monogatari*, 1953). Although it is less playful than most of his other films, *Tokyo Story* is typical of Ozu in its seeming simplicity, its reserve and deep compassion. Ozu noted it was one of his most melodramatic films, but to Western eyes it is rigorously subtle and restrained. Even so, no one questions its profound emotional power.

There is more to be said about Ozu's comic sensibility. He began in the silent era (he was still making silent films up to 1936), and was an admirer of Lubitsch and Chaplin. His silents are predominantly light comedies, more dynamic and exuberant than the later work, but already tempered by the keen emotional sensitivity, which would mark him as a true Chekhovian, and one of very finest film-makers of the twentieth century.

> **180-DEGREE LINE**
> The accepted convention that a scene should be shot from the same side, so that a character does not switch from screen left to screen right between cuts.

The Essentialist

Roberto Rossellini

Neo-realism was born in the ruins of Mussolini's Italy. The movement produced several important film-makers, but Roberto Rossellini became the figurehead. Championed by André Bazin, his films had a radical impact on the French *nouvelle vague* (see page 86).

Born 1906, Rome, Italy
Importance Leader of the neo-realist movement in Italy
Died 1977, Rome, Italy

Mussolini's fascist regime had been in power for nearly 20 years – all Rossellini's adult life – when Roberto entered the film industry as an apprentice. His first three features were necessarily made under the auspices of the government and the censorship that came with it, but it is somewhat misleading to call them 'fascist propaganda'.

His fourth film, *Rome, Open City* (*Roma, Città Aperta* 1945) is usually referred to as the first neo-realist film, although De Sica's *Ossessione* (1942), an unauthorised translation of James M Cain's *The Postman Always Rings Twice*, shares some of the same attributes: proletarian milieu, location shooting and a more realistic, psychological approach to sex and violence.

Shot mostly on the streets, with a hand-held camera and using whatever stock Rossellini could get, *Rome, Open City* garnered international attention, winning the best-film award at

'I'm not trying to solve the problems of the world. I'm a man of the world, and I want to be present.'

the Cannes Film Festival. Rossellini had set out to make a documentary about a priest in the Resistance, but the project evolved into an intense, authentic drama as the underground war waged on.

Paisà (1946) comprises six episodes from across the country to convey the experience of the liberation. The use of non-professional actors and documentary elements complied with the writer Cesare

Zavattini's neo-realist manifesto, which called for film-makers to confront the audience with their reality.

Germany Year Zero (1958) is an even more desolate record of the times, this time shot in what remained of Berlin. At a time when almost all Western cinema was largely confined to studio sets and largely in thrall to glamour and escapism, Rossellini's neo-realist trilogy opened the eyes of many film-makers – including the actress Ingrid Bergman, who was so moved by his films she wrote and volunteered her services.

The critic Laura Mulvey called Viaggio in Italia *(1954) 'the first modern film'.*

The couple, who were both married, caused a scandal when they became lovers, and the public rejected the six films they made together, including *Stromboli* (1950) and *Viaggio in Italia* (*Journey to Italy*, 1954). By now Rossellini had split from the neo-realist Marxist doctrines to pursue his own ideas about spirituality and cinema.

Virtually plotless, *Viaggio in Italia* follows a bickering married couple – George Sanders and Bergman – as they drive through the Italian countryside. Rossellini reveals theme and character not through melodrama, but through the camera's precise delineation of the characters in their environment. Antonioni, Godard, Scorsese, François Truffaut, Bernardo Bertolucci and Pier Paolo Pasolini have all acknowledged the importance of this work on their own.

GENRE

**The conventions of genre film-making fell into place quickly
– there were genre films before there were film stars. For
producers, the genre picture was first and foremost an
organising principle, a way to assemble a film and market it
to a specific audience. Film-goers appreciate the continuity
represented by genre, as well as variations within the
established codes.**

The most popular Hollywood genres include the crime film,
musicals, comedy, westerns, melodrama, science fiction, horror
and the biopic – but there are subdivisions (screwball comedy;
slapstick; romantic comedy) and cross-pollination between them
(the horror comedy).

Genre is determined by iconography, milieu, character and plot,
and also, often, by the presence of familiar stars and cinematic tropes.
The western, for example, very often begins with a long shot
establishing the arid landscape typical of the American West, and a
cowboy riding in the distance. The score is usually symphonic or a
traditional folk ballad. The drama will most often be a morality tale,
and the genre carries expectations of violent confrontation (the gun
fight) and virile action.

If auteurist criticism champions the individual artist (see page
26), genre criticism examines films as symptomatic of wider cultural
concerns. By examining the assumptions and conventions that many
westerns share, critics can point to prevalent sociological, ideological
and psychological fixations; the idea of frontier, for example,
civilisation poised against the wilderness, and how that relates to
America's sense of itself.

The gangster film can be seen as a rebuke to the autonomy
enshrined in the western: 'the gangster is the "no" to that great

American "yes", which is stamped so big over our official culture,' wrote Robert Warshow in his essay 'The Gangster as Tragic Hero' (1970). In his pursuit of material success at any cost, the gangster is a quintessential individualist, a grotesque paragon of the American Dream destined for a spectacular fall in the last reel.

Other industrial film centres – such as Tokyo, Hong Kong and Mumbai – have also produced a preponderance of genre films, in some cases similar to American models, in others quite distinctive. In Japan we find the samurai film, which is deeply rooted in historical tradition but also parallels the American western so closely that Kurosawa's *Seven Samurai* easily became John Sturges' *The Magnificent Seven*. On the other hand, there is no Hollywood equivalent of the '*shomingeki*', a popular genre of serio-comedies about the lower-middle classes that produced some of the finest Japanese films.

While most Hollywood genres have proved surprisingly durable, their popularity waxes and wanes and their dynamics have altered with the times – offering sociologists more room for speculation. The brief blooming of the literally dark, claustrophobic and cynical crime thrillers French critics dubbed 'film noir' in the war and immediate post-war years, is often attributed to factors like the disillusionment of returning veterans, and their ambivalence about the work – and play – women had been up to on the home front.

Similarly, there was a vogue for conspiracy and paranoia thrillers in the early 1970s, perhaps reflecting public anxieties around the assassinations of John and Robert Kennedy and Martin Luther King; the Nixon administration and Watergate break-in. The same era brought a crop of 'revisionist'

> *'All you need to make a movie is a girl and a gun,'*
>
> Jean-Luc Godard

westerns, dirtier and more realistic, consciously revoking the romantic myths of the 1930s and 1940s. Later, the *Star Wars* films also drew on Western archetypes, this time to reassert the pleasures of escapism. In these ways genre mutates and sets up its own on-going dialectic.

Akira Kurosawa

Japan's most celebrated film-maker, Akira Kurosawa alerted Western audiences to the existence of Asian cinema when *Rashomon* won the Golden Lion at the Venice Film Festival in 1951. His bold, muscular storytelling and flamboyant mise-en-scène (see page 11) were readily appreciated, especially in his samurai dramas and Shakespearean adaptations.

Born 1910, Tokyo, Japan
Importance An influential director of action sequences during the 1950s and 1960s
Died 1998, Tokyo, Japan

Kurosawa never shied away from the big themes: mortality, war and existential despair. Scenes of carnage and mass destruction crop up in many of his films. Nevertheless, he is a humanist who regards these horrors with compassion, and a progressive who engages with the social issues of his day: corporate corruption in *The Bad Sleep Well* (1960); the atom bomb in *I Live in Fear* (1955); civic responsibility in *Ikiru* (1952); ecology in *Dersu Uzala* (1975). With few exceptions these are films of ethical enquiry and moral seriousness, often starring his favourite actor, Toshiro Mifune (with whom he had 16 collaborations in all).

Kurosawa was well versed in Western literature and film. Military censors complained that his first film, *Sugata Sanshiro* (1943), was 'too British-American', a complaint that would resurface over the years. Several of Kurosawa's films would be remade as westerns, including the masterly *Seven Samurai* (1954), which became *The Magnificent Seven*, and the entertainment *Yojimbo* (1961) which inspired Sergio Leone's *A Fistful of Dollars* (1964).

Pioneering the use of multiple cameras for battle sequences, and adopting the telephoto lens to achieve a more visceral impact, Kurosawa was probably the foremost director of action sequences in the 1950s and early 1960s. In this capacity he influenced many US film-makers, including George Lucas, who borrowed from *The*

Hidden Fortress (1958) when he made *Star Wars* (1977). Repaying the debt, Lucas and Francis Coppola would enable Kurosawa to make *Kagemusha* (1980) when he could no longer find financing in Japan.

He transposed Shakespeare to medieval Japan and seamlessly integrated elements of Noh theatre in his *Macbeth – Throne of Blood* (1957); and *King Lear – Ran* (1985). Dispensing with Shakespearean verse, Kurosawa staged these tragedies with such a keen eye for men's most destructive compulsions that it scarcely seems a sacrifice. *Ran* – meaning 'chaos' – is one of the most spectacular colour films ever made, even as it edges towards pageantry.

Kurosawa's superb visuals are tied to self-conscious literary values in a way that makes the films more readily accessible than other Japanese masters like Yasujiro Ozu, Kenji Mizoguchi and Mikio Naruse, but which also limits them. For all his breadth and scope, Kurosawa's preordained and omniscient viewpoint can slide into hollow overstatement and sentimental bluster. He remains a master film-maker, but a classicist rooted in the traditions of the nineteenth and first half of the twentieth century.

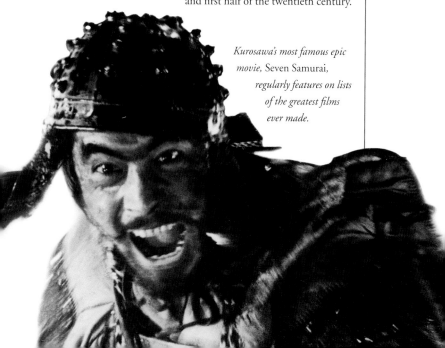

Kurosawa's most famous epic movie, Seven Samurai, *regularly features on lists of the greatest films ever made.*

Robert Bresson

Robert Bresson rejected conventional movies as filmed theatre. The art of what he called the '_cinématographe_' was to film nothing but the essential. For many, Bresson is the most radical modern film-maker, the artist who broke from classical 'invisible' editing to open up a wider dialectic with an active spectator.

Born 1901, Auvergne, France
Importance Made a radical departure from conventional film-making
Died 1999, Paris, France

Despite his iconoclasm, Bresson was a narrative film-maker – indeed his storytelling is conspicuously linear and realistic, whether it concerns a prison break – _A Man Escaped_ (1956); the fate of a donkey – _Au Hasard, Balthazar_ (1966); or the circulation of a forged 500-franc note – _L'argent_ (1983).

His first films were relatively conventional, but by his third feature, _Diary of a Country Priest_ (_Journal d'un Curé de Campagne_, 1951), Bresson was beginning the process of critical distillation that would define his work. He began to cast non-actors – like a painter, he called them 'models' – and drained them of expression to escape the simulation that professional actors are trained in. And he started to explore off-screen space with greater acuity than perhaps any film-maker before him: the soundtrack creates the environment but the camera concentrates our gaze elsewhere. His compositions are neutral – he used a 50mm lens and preferred static medium shots with minimal lighting effects. Their meaning derives from juxtaposition and duration, although it's up to the spectator to supply it.

The critical buzz words around Bresson are austerity and transcendence. Neither is entirely true, for there is something very sensual about his strategy of repression allayed, from time to time, by the reprieve of the close-up, or perhaps a burst of classical music. This music, emanating from outside the film's plot, may signal divine grace or spiritual transcendence – Bresson was brought up a Jansenist (a branch of catholicism emphasizing the concept of original sin and predestination) – but salvation is never a *fait accompli*, and the film-maker's religious conviction remains an open question.

Under the opening credits of *Au Hasard, Balthazar*, Bresson interrupts Schubert with the braying of a donkey, and both realities carry equal weight. In this simple but moving fable, he presents a base and prevalent evil, yet illuminates it in shafts of innocence and grace. Loved and petted in childhood, then quickly put to hard labour, the eponymous ass endures violent abuse, indifference and neglect at the hands of men driven by pride, cruelty and greed. Is this creature a Christ figure, or do we invest our compassion in a dumb animal?

Bresson's minimalism did not find favour with large audiences, and his output was restricted to just 13 features over 40 years. Yet Bresson's epigrammatic book, *Notes on Cinematography*, is a key text to many film-makers, and his influence has been immense: on Jean-Luc Godard, certainly, Maurice Pialat and Jacques Rivette, as well as Antonioni, Tarkovsky, and a later generation of film-makers stretching from Jim Jarmusch in the US, to Finland's Aki Kaurismaki and Jia Zhangke in China.

Few film-makers have been able to approach Bresson's purity or his emotional impact as a director.

The Modernist

Michelangelo Antonioni

Abandonment, alienation and ambiguity are the recurring themes in Michelangelo Antonioni's cinema, characteristics of modernist art – and twentieth-century life – that led him to carve out a new architecture of cinematic space and time. Arguably the most imposing of the great modernists, Antonioni married philosophical contemplation to an aesthetic always on the cusp of abstract pictorialism.

Born 1912, Ferrara, Italy
Importance One of the most accomplished modernist directors
Died 2007, Rome, Italy

Antonioni's first five features are melodramas with a strong neo-realist flavour, and fine films in their own right. But the sixth, *L'Avventura* (1960), is a landmark film, and was immediately recognised as such. In 1962, the critics polled by the magazine, *Sight & Sound*, ranked it the second greatest film ever made.

A film about the disappearance of a young woman on a boating trip in the Mediterranean, and the search conducted by her best friend and her lover, *L'Avventura* dared to leave the plot hanging. We never discover what happened to Anna, though various alternatives are suggested. This isn't simply withholding narrative information, it's a completely different way of looking at the world.

Antonioni's camera places figures in a landscape, not against a backdrop. Often we feel space engulfs character, not least because character is more difficult to identify; people act in ambiguous and seemingly contradictory ways. They may not know themselves. Little is spoken, we are invited to

'The cinema today should be tied to truth rather than logic... And the truth of our daily lives is neither mechanical, conventional, nor artificial, as stories usually are.'

78 79

scrutinise gestures, reactions, silences. Events occur, but the director does not construct his scenes to explain them.

Antonioni developed these ideas in a string of modern masterpieces: *La Notte* (1961); *L'Eclisse* (1962); *The Red Desert* (1964); and the Swinging London thriller *Blowup* (1966). This was an extraordinary time in film, when auteurs like Antonioni, Bergman, Fellini and Godard were cultural touchstones for a generation of dedicated cinephiles. Thus Antonioni was able to work with film stars – including Monica Vitti, Marcello Mastroianni, Jeanne Moreau, Alain Delon, Richard Harris and Jack Nicholson – and command the kind of budgets that enabled him to, for example, paint entire fields the exact hue he wanted (in *The Red Desert*, his first colour film).

Antonioni had an international box-office hit with *Blowup*, an satire of 1960s hedonism and a murder mystery that morphed into a self-reflexive impasse. Invited to Hollywood, he clearly conveyed his disgust with materialism in *Zabriskie Point* (1970), but his mise-en-scène (see page 11) felt mannered. He rallied with *The Passenger* (1974), and showed flashes of the old brilliance thereafter. A stroke in 1985 left him partially paralysed and all but mute, yet he wrote and co-directed *Beyond the Clouds* (1995) and a segment in the 2004 portmanteau, *Eros*.

Antonioni was noted for his use of long takes; colour was also an integral part of his cinematic style.

Ingmar Bergman

No film-maker wrestled more painfully with the knowledge of his own mortality than Ingmar Bergman. His father was a Lutheran minister, and he cast a long shadow over Bergman's films, including his premature swansong, *Fanny and Alexander* (1982), and perhaps his purest masterpiece, *Winter Light* (1962).

Born 1918, Uppsala, Sweden
Importance Tremendously successful European art-house director
Died 2007, Faro, Sweden

Bergman's anguished introspection permeated his films, the great majority of which he wrote himself. When they weren't directly concerned with religion, the films were still preoccupied with existential doubt that gnawed at strained family relationships, bitter marriages and passionate, but ultimately unfulfilling love affairs. The playwrights August Strindberg and Henrik Ibsen were probably the most

Scenes from a Marriage, *starring Liv Ullmann, was originally a TV mini-series spanning 295 minutes. It was cut down to 168 minutes for cinematic release.*

important artistic influences on his work, along with the Scandinavian film-makers Carl Dreyer and Victor Sjöström.

What's remarkable today is the extent to which this austere and uncompromising artist made such a deep imprint on late-twentieth-century Western culture. Arguably Rossellini and Renoir had a more enduring impact on the way films are made, but in Bergman's lifetime only Kurosawa and Fellini spoke so directly to international audiences and film-makers. Among his many honours, Bergman was nominated for nine Academy Awards. In 1997, at a ceremony for the 50th anniversary of the Cannes Film Festival, he was awarded 'the Palm of Palms', a reflection of his unique standing in world cinema.

Although his career stretches back to 1946, he hit his stride with *Summer with Monika* in 1953, and came to international attention with the uncharacteristically charming sex comedy *Smiles of a Summer Night* in 1955. This was succeeded by the medieval allegory *The Seventh Seal* (1957), *Wild Strawberries* (1957) and *The Magician* (1958). A couple of years later, his loosely grouped 'Silence of God' trilogy cemented his standing as the most philosophically rigorous of European art-house directors. *Persona* (1966) is his most overt modernist text, and ranked fifth in the 1972 *Sight & Sound* magazine critics' poll for the best films ever made. A year later, he made two more psychological masterpieces, *Cries and Whispers* and *Scenes from a Marriage*.

Bergman suffered a nervous breakdown after being arrested for tax evasion and retired from cinema in 1982, although he continued to write scripts for television and proved he hadn't mellowed any when he was persuaded to direct *Saraband* in 2003. The inherently theatrical 'high seriousness' for which he stands is no longer fashionable in the age of irony and postmodernism, and some of his later work is painfully self-conscious, even torpid.

But Bergman was more than his cariacature. As a director, his collaboration with cinematographer Sven Nykvist ran the gamut from searing expressionism to scenes of graceful, limpid natural light. He was a searching, fearless dramatist who held himself to the highest standards as an artist.

Federico Fellini

A titan of European art cinema, Federico Fellini was a flamboyant figure whose unashamedly personal films have a carnivalesque quality. They include *La Strada* (1954), *La Dolce Vita* (1961) and *8¹/₂* (1963), the last being one of the most influential films about film-making and a landmark in modernist cinema.

Born 1920, Rimini, Italy
Importance Hugely influential director of exuberant, self-reflexive films
Died 1993, Rome, Italy

Fellini started writing screenplays in the early 1940s, most notably for Rossellini's neo-realist classics *Roma, Città Aperta* and *Paisà* (1946). The collaboration continued as both men moved away from the strict tenets of that movement, first with an episode in *L'Amore* (1948) about a peasant woman who believes the tramp who impregnated her is St Joseph, and then *Francis, God's Jester* (1950).

Fellini began directing in 1950 with *Lights of Variety*, but it was *La Strada* (Film number 4½) that put him on the map, a heartbreaking poetic fable starring his wife, Giulietta Masina. Although the visual style is humble compared with later films, it marks the first step away from realism. Strong elements of social satire endured, along with Fellini's controversial brand of Catholicism. The fragile, but plucky, Masina would prove an important muse; she would star in several of his best-known films, including *Cabiria* (1957) and *Juliet of the Spirits* (1965).

As Italy (or more precisely, Rome) moved towards a more affluent lifestyle, Fellini reflected the change. *La Dolce Vita* is a rolling panorama of a debauched, new, high society of film stars, models and tabloid reporters. (This is the picture that gave us the word 'papparazzi'.) Fellini announces his intentions with an audacious opening shot: a helicopter lifting a statue of Christ up and out of the city of Rome.

The handsome, elegant Mastroianni became the director's alter ego in the second half of his career, launched by the brilliant *8½*, an autobiographical fantasy about a film-maker mired in a creative impasse. Here, for the first time, Fellini dove into his dreams as a source of psychological self-analysis and baroque, extravagant imagery. It's at this point that Fellini films become *sui generis*, or unmistakably 'Felliniesque', an adjective inspired by his exuberant, if often grotesque and surreal, imagery.

For some critics, Fellini's subsequent immersion in a cinema of imaginative spectacle and orgiastic tableaux with *Fellini Satyricon* (1969), *Roma* (1972) and *City of Women* (1980) represents a retreat into self-indulgence and visual bombast. Others celebrate the free-associative nature of these episodic, non-linear films, their bold, original visuals and Jungian candour. The evocative film, *Amarcord* (also known as *I Remember*, 1973), inspired by Fellini's memories of his childhood in Rimini, stands out for its warmth and subtlety.

Screen siren Anita Eckberg cavorts in the Trevi Fountain, Rome, in Fellini's La Dolce Vita *(1961).*

Fellini was one of a kind and clearly inimitable, yet, by daring to dissect his own psyche on screen, and with such aplomb, he was an inspiration to many film-makers, including Woody Allen, Terry Gilliam, Andy Warhol, Tim Burton, Emir Kusturica, Martin Scorsese, and Francis Coppola (who employed Fellini's favourite composer, Nino Rota, to score *The Godfather*).

India's Supreme Film-maker

Satyajit Ray

A prolific film-maker, Satyajit Ray made 37 features as writer and director in 36 years. His work takes in every strata of Bengali society, from peasant life to that of the upper classes, and he approached each of them with a profound humanism.

Born 1921, Calcutta, India
Importance Raised the status of Indian film to equal that of China and Japan
Died 1992, Calcutta, India

Like Kurosawa, Ray widened the world view of occidental cinephiles naive in their assumption of cultural superiority. He came from a cultured Bengali household. His father and his grandfather were both writers, and the writer Tagore was a close friend of the family. Educated in Bengali and English, Ray studied science and economics in Calcutta, then went to Tagore's rural university in Shantiniketan to study fine arts, where he was immersed in Indian and Far Eastern art. Although he gravitated towards Western classical music and Hollywood movies, Ray stressed that, as a film-maker, he was as much the product of Shantiniketan. The tensions between tradition and modernity that go hand in hand with colonialism and development are central to many of his films.

'It is the kind of cinema that flows with the serenity and nobility of a big river'

Akira Kurosawa

In 1944, he was asked to illustrate a 1930s Bengali novel, *Pather Panchali* ('Song of the Road'), the story of a peasant family and the travails of Apu, the son who eventually quits the village for the town. Seven years later – encouraged by a meeting with Jean Renoir on *The River* in 1949 – Ray set out to make this his first film. It was an arduous, three-year process, financed in part by the sale of his record collection and his wife's jewellery, but when *Pather Panchali* screened at the Cannes Film Festival in 1956, Ray was immediately recognised as a new master. It was enough, at any rate, to allow him to give up his day job in an advertising company.

If the Apu trilogy suggested Ray was a neo-realist, it soon became apparent that he was more concerned with the poetic expression of emotion than documenting poverty. Partly for budgetary reasons, many of his films are chamber pieces, domestic comedies and melodramas with a contemporary setting. Ray was particularly sensitive to the compromised position of women in India. In *Devi* (*The Goddess*, 1960) a young woman comes to believe she is the reincarnation of the goddess Kali. In *Mahanagar* (*The Big City*, 1963) a lower-middle-class wife takes a job to the consternation of her extended family. And in arguably his finest film, *Charulata* (*The Lonely Wife*, 1964), a nineteenth-century wife becomes disillusioned with her neglectful husband and falls in love with his cousin, foolishly believing that he sees her for herself.

Ray suffered a heart attack during the making of *Home and the World* (1984). His last few films have a more prosaic, functional style, but still evince his fascination with shifting value systems, integrity, corruption and disillusionment.

Despite the leisurely tempo of his observational character pieces, Ray produced his films at an impressive pace.

NEW WAVES

The decade from 1958 to 1968 brought revolutionary change. It was a generational shift, most dramatic in France, where the *nouvelle vague* ('new wave') broke through in significant numbers, inspiring young film-makers with a fresh approach and new ideas. Kindred movements sprung up in Eastern Europe, Italy, Germany, Spain, the UK and Japan.

The prosperity of the times liberated young people from the struggles their parents and grandparents had experienced. It was a period of tumultuous social change and intense political divisions made manifest in the Berlin Wall. Existentialism was in the air, and intellectual debate flourished in the universities and cafes of Europe. It was in Paris, especially, that an intense, passionate cinephilia took root, facilitated by the archives established by Henri Langlois at the Cinématheque Française, and fanned by André Bazin's magazine *Cahiers du Cinéma*.

Obsessed with American cinema and virulently opposed to the conservative 'quality' film-making coming out of France at the time, the *Cahiers* critics insisted that cinema should represent the personal expression of the director – so it was natural they should gravitate to directing themselves (see Auteurism, page 26).

François Truffaut's first film, the autobiographical *The 400 Blows* (*Les Quatre Cents Coups*) won the Palme d'Or at the 1959 Cannes Film Festival, exactly a year after he had been banned from attending as a critic because of his withering appraisal of the French selections. He was 27 years old.

His colleagues Jean Luc Godard, Eric Rohmer, Jacques Rivette and Claude Chabrol all made their first features between 1958 and 1960. Their compatriots included Agnes Varda, whose debut *La Pointe Courte* (1954) was inspired by William Faulkner, Picasso, and

Brecht; Alain Resnais (*Night and Fog*; *Hiroshima Mon Amour*); Chris Marker (*Le Joli Mai*) and Jacques Demy (*Lola*).

Varda's example was important, not just because it was a modernist work, but because, at 26, she was unschooled in film-making, and because it was made as a cooperative venture with an unpaid cast and crew. In other words, Varda showed that you didn't have to serve an apprenticeship: anyone could make a film.

> *'Photography is truth. And cinema is truth twenty-four times a second.'*
>
> Jean-Luc Godard

The *nouvelle vague* film-makers capitalised on lighter, more portable 16mm cameras that became more widely available in the 1950s and that facilitated hand-held, documentary-style shooting. Despite their respect for Hollywood, they didn't attempt to duplicate the glossy American style, rather they borrowed generic and stylistic tropes and shook them up, incorporating jarring dislocations and mood swings, throwing snippets of documentary and slapstick up against romance and tragedy. It was at once eclectic and iconoclastic.

The same impulses inspired young film-makers everywhere: in Poland, Roman Polanski and Andrei Wajda; in Czechoslovakia, Milos Forman and Ivan Passer; in Hungary, Miklos Jancso; in Greece, Theo Angelopoulos; in Italy, Pier Paolo Pasolini and Bernardo Bertolucci; in Britain, Lindsay Anderson; in Japan, Nagisa Oshima; in Brazil, Glauber Rocha… Only the US and the Soviet Union remained impervious, but Hollywood began to crumble as the 1960s wore on.

These breaking new waves could not stay new forever and, by 1970, the tide had started to turn. The mainstream effectively co-opted or marginalised these radical film-makers and their cinematic rhetoric. In 1973, Jean Eustache made *The Mother and the Whore*, a wrenching elegy for the squandered ideals of *nouvelle vague* and the crippled Marxist politics in which it became entwined – yet the film itself embodies much of what is of lasting value in the movement: spontaneity, intellectual passion and, sometimes, searing honesty.

Jean-Luc Godard

**The most innovative, restless and radical of the French
nouvelle vague (see page 86) directors who emerged in the
late 1950s and shook up international cinema, Jean-Luc
Godard is a Brechtian who constantly reframes
the relationship between the spectator and the
spectacle. This, in turn, has made him a polarising
figure, revered for his early work, but too
'problematic' for contemporary acceptance.**

Born 1930, Paris, France
Importance A seminal
director of the French
nouvelle vague

Like François Truffaut, Eric Rohmer, Claude Chabrol and Jacques
Rivette, Godard was a critic for *Cahiers du Cinéma* magazine in the
1950s, an ardent auteurist who championed Nicholas Ray and
Roberto Rossellini among others. His first feature, *A Bout de Souffle*
(*Breathless*, 1959) is a rude, anarchic, nihilistic sketch of an insolent,
doomed-to-die young hoodlum. Godard's jerky, bebop rhythms, his
street-smart, hand-held camera and his penchant for lofty
philosophical dialogue and low-brow pulp action all signalled
an exciting, new direction in film-making.

Godard shot off 15 features and seven 'sketches' (contributions to
portmanteau films) between 1960 and 1967. True to his declaration
that 'all you need to make a movie is a girl and a gun', there always is
a girl – usually Anna Karina – and although the films don't all feature
guns, intellectual fireworks are guaranteed, as he shuffles through
politics, pop and a dizzying array of filmic styles with impetuous
abandon. One minute he's trying his hand at a neo-realist musical
(*Une Femme est une Femme*, 1961), the next a sci-fi mystery thriller
shot entirely in contemporary Paris (*Alphaville*, 1965).

Le Mépris (*Contempt*, 1963) is a key text, a free take on Alberto
Moravia's novel, with Michel Piccoli as a French screenwriter
collaborating on a film of *The Odyssey* to be directed by Fritz Lang.

Godard's only US co-production, it allowed him to thrash out his very mixed feelings about the Hollywood tradition he loved and meant to bury. Defiantly classicist in content, radically innovative in form, right from the spoken opening credits, *Le Mépris* represents Godard's signature uneasy marriage of the sensual and the cerebral.

After *Pierrot le Fou* (1965) Godard turned the page on *nouvelle vague* with *Week-end* (1967). This angry, Buñuelian assault on the bourgeoisie ends in a revolutionary bloodbath, cannibalism and 'the end of cinema'. Godard's so-called Maoist period – roughly 1968 to 1973, is dogmatic, uncompromising and, if not unwatchable, then largely unseen (then and now).

He made a number of ambitious dialectical essays for French television before returning to cinema with *Sauve Qui Peut – la Vie* (*Slow Motion*, 1980), his 'second first film', which began a more lyrical, interrogative phase. While his erratic later films have not had the international distribution of his new-wave days, he remains a challenging artist on the vanguard of debates on the politics of cinematic discourse.

His massive eight-part, five-hour *Histoire(s) du Cinéma* is a subjective, free-associative epitaph for the art form held up against the mirror of twentieth-century wars, atrocities and capitalist imperialism. Almost impenetrably dense, the collection stands as the director's magnum opus and proof that, whatever else he accomplished, Godard remained a film critic throughout his career.

Jean-Paul Belmondo played the eponymous hero in Pierrot le Fou *(1965). The film was a summation of everything Godard had achieved with* nouvelle vague.

The Mystic

Andrei Tarkovsky

With their brooding, poetic imagery and hypnotic transfixion on duration, films like *Andrei Rublev*, *Stalker* and *Mirror* stand at the opposite end of the spectrum from Hollywood entertainment. Among Russia's most acclaimed film-makers, Tarkovksy was a profoundly spiritual artist searching for moments of divine mystery and illumination.

Born 1932, Zavrazhye, Soviet Union
Importance The leading Soviet film-maker of the Cold War period
Died 1986, Paris, France

Tarkovsky was not a political film-maker, but he had a troubled relationship with the Soviet authorities. His second feature, *Andrei Rublev* (1966) was suppressed for several years. The epic (and largely invented) account of a medieval Russian icon painter who takes a monastic vow of silence during his travels through a country beset by wars, paganism and suffering was such a fervid, potent demonstration of the director's veneration of Mother Russia, God and art that the communists scarcely knew what to do with it. Yet the audacity and virtuosity of this masterwork could not be ignored. Tarkovsky acknowledged Kurosawa as an influence on the way he filmed the elements: water and rain, mud, fog and fire are an omnipresent reality in his vision; so too, animals. 'A film of the earth', he called it. It's also a brutally violent picture.

But Tarkovsky is no realist; the emphasis on nature, tumult and entropy fuels the search for inner peace. His pictures are both austere, in terms of narrative information and rich, in terms of their dense, enigmatic and poetic imagery. The prologue of *Andrei Rublev* is an allegory involving an early (doomed) fifteenth-century balloon flight – an episode we're invited to interpret as a kind of religious affront (or not), but also to share as a heady, exhilarating experience.

Tarkovsky's long, slow, sinuous tracking shots create a space for contemplation, even meditation. He called his book on the art of

film-making *Sculpting in Time*.
The longer he made films, the
longer these takes became. In
Nostalgia (made in exile, in
Italy in 1983) a man walks the
length of an empty swimming
pool with a lighted candle,
but is forced to begin again
and again when the candle
blows out before his pilgrimage
is complete. Tarkovksy films
this in a single take, and the
sequence derives its power from
the understanding that the shot
is also a kind of pilgrimage.

If the Soviet system
restricted Tarkovsky's career –
he completed only seven
features between 1962 and his
death in 1986, the last two of
them in exile in the West – it's
unlikely he would have thrived
in a commercial context. Nor is

*Tarkovsky rejected the common
observation that he was a 'symbolist',
arguing that symbols reduce complex
metaphors to simplistic meanings.*

it possible to extricate him from his roots in Soviet culture. He was
disparaging about genre and dismissive of most film-makers outside
his pantheon of 'poets': Bresson, above all; Dovzhenko, Antonioni,
Mizoguchi, Bergman, Kurosawa and few others. Few would question
his place alongside them. The philosophical science-fiction *Solaris*
(1972) was a riposte of sorts to Kubrick's *2001: A Space Odyssey*
(1968); and *The Sacrifice* (1986) a self-conscious last testament;
but *Mirror* (1974), an autobiographical, stream-of-consciousness
reflection on childhood, family, memory and metaphysics, may be
his masterpiece.

Rainer Werner Fassbinder

Fassbinder was the most driven and dynamic of a passionate group of post-war German film-makers who emerged in the 1960s and early 1970s. Bisexual and leftwing, Fassbinder was typical of his generation in his love for classical Hollywood, and his cinema marries that mode with radical politics, stinging social criticism and searing psychological candour.

Born 1945, Bavaria, Germany
Importance The dynamo of the New German Cinema
Died 1982, Munich, Germany

The New German Cinema was just one of the national film movements that rippled out across Europe from the seismic generational shift enacted by the French *nouvelle vague* (see page 86). In Germany, the shambolic state of a once-proud film industry, the guilty inheritance of Nazism, and the stark contrast between the booming materialism of the West with the Communist regime in the East all fuelled a turbulent, radical mood.

Brought up by a divorcee (a translator, she appeared in many of her son's films under her maiden name, Lilo Pempelt) Fassbinder was a film-school reject who got caught up in Munich's bohemian underground theatre scene. There, he quickly became the focal point for an extended family of actors.

Inspired by Godard, Straub and Brecht, Fassbinder started with bare bones, localised deconstructions on American genre pictures: gangster films, and even a western. But it was when he turned to melodrama that everything clicked. Fassbinder was a devoted admirer of the German-born Hollywood director Douglas Sirk, whose opulent 1950s' weepies indicted empty materialism through a flagrantly expressive mise-en-scène.

In films like *The Merchant of Four Seasons* (1972) and *Fear Eats the Soul* (1974), Fassbinder stripped away Hollywood glitz for social realism. His heroes were outsiders, excluded from the country's riches, patronised and exploited by the middle class. If the politics are uncompromising, the dramas find their emotional truth in the cruel sadomasochistic power games lying at the heart of almost all Fassbinder's sexual relationships.

With *The Marriage of Maria Braun* (1979) and *Lola* (1981) he turned his attention to enterprising, self-made women, apparent winners in Konrad Adenaur's 'Economic Miracle' of the 1950s, this time in the lush, saturated Sirkian style. Played by Hanna Schygulla and Barbara Sukowa, these women flourish through hard graft (Fassbinder's governing metaphor for capitalist exchange is prostitution) but bourgeois morality prevents them from enjoying the fruits of their labour. Taken with *Berlin Alexanderplatz, Lili Marleen* (1981) and *Veronika Voss* (1982), these later films constitute an ambitious attempt to trace the psychology of Germany through the twentieth century, filtered through the cultural idioms of the time.

It's impossible to know where this prodigious talent would have gone from here. The New German Cinema petered out in the 1980s, and many of its leading lights headed for the US. Fassbinder died of heart failure related to his drug use in 1982 at the age of 37.

Fassbinder was noted for his astonishing productivity. Between 1968 and his untimely death in 1982, he wrote and directed 41 feature-length films for cinema and television, including the 15½ hour mini-series Berlin Alexanderplatz *(1980).*

The Philosopher

Krzysztof Kieslowski

For almost a decade, from the late 1980s to his death in 1996, Kieslowski assumed the mantle of standard bearer for the European art film, the heir to Bergman and Tarkovsky. After the collapse of the Iron Curtain he graduated from astringent ethical dramas in the Polish suburbs to grand, visually ostentatious philosophical abstractions based in Paris.

Born 1941, Warsaw, Poland
Importance Leading director of European art films in the late-twentieth century
Died 1996, Warsaw, Poland

Kieslowski's first films were documentaries, and inherently critical of a Communist state that fostered propaganda and ignored reality ('The Communist world described how it should be and not how it really was', he said.) However he became increasingly concerned with the ethics of representing – and interfering in – other lives, a quandary reflected at the end of his breakthrough fiction film, *Camera Buff* (1979), when the eponymous hero finally turns the camera on himself.

Kieslowski's fiction films reveal a gradual alienation from politics, and a growing fascination with fate, personal morality and metaphysical questions. In *Blind Chance* (1981) a seemingly random occurrence at a train station affects the political future of a young medical student who, in different strands, either catches, or fails to catch, a train to Warsaw. Narrated by a recently deceased lawyer, *No End* (1984) was Kieslowski's first film with regular collaborators co-writer Krzysztof Piesiewicz and composer Zbigniew Preisner, a kind of ghost story hinging on a political prosecution.

But it was *The Decalogue* (1988) that made his international reputation. Ten hour-long films made for Polish television and inspired by the Ten Commandments, *The Decalogue* is a series of austere, rigorous ethical dramas, set on the same dismal Warsaw

Three Colours: Red *(1994), Kieslowski's final film, confirmed the trilogy's commercial and critical success around the world.*

housing estate but photographed by nine different cinematographers. He expanded two into feature length films but seen together, these taut, subtle, twisty episodes assume greater resonance, as characters from one story rub shoulders with people from another. Kieslowski would pursue this idea of interconnectedness in his first international co-production, *The Double Life of Veronique* (1991) and his *Three Colour* trilogy, *Blue* (1993), *White* (1994) and *Red* (1994). In these films, he adopts a rich cinematic vocabulary, playing with colour schema, macro-close-ups suggestive of interior reveries, magisterial camera moves and rhapsodic bursts of Preisner's orchestral music.

Ostensibly based on the colours of the French flag and the revolutionary ideals of liberty, equality and freedom, each individual film explores these themes in the context of personal relationships, even as Kieslowski weaves together a magnificent tapestry that pulls all three together. Kieslowski announced his retirement from film-making shortly after completing the trilogy, and died two years later.

Abbas Kiarostami

Neo-realism and postmodernism are not obvious bedfellows, but they combine convincingly in the spare, elliptical, philosophical films of Abbas Kiarostami. Working under heavily proscribed conditions in Iran, Kiarostami developed a minimalist style, juxtaposing long, observational takes with omission and restraint.

Born 1940, Tehran, Iran
Importance Leading director of Iran's new-wave cinema

A latecomer to the Iranian New Wave that took shape in the 1960s and 1970s, Kiarostami did not receive international attention until the late 1980s, by which time he was operating under the censorious Islamic regime of the Ayatollahs, which prohibited numerous staples of cinematic entertainment, including relatively mild instances of sex and violence, and also shielded local film-makers and audiences from 'corrupt' and 'decadent' foreign influences. Kiarostami is not alone among his compatriots in his fondness for child protagonists, realistic milieux and simple, but oblique, allegorical narratives. Such strategies afford a measure of authenticity without baiting the censors.

Kiarostami's work with children goes back to the 1960s, when he helped establish a film department at the Institute for the Intellectual Development of Children and Young Adults (which he ran from 1969 to 1974). Child protagonists crop up in his first feature, *The Traveller* (1974) and *Where is the Friend's Home?* (1987). They are the subject of the documentaries *Homework* (1989) and *ABC Africa* (2001), and the first chapter of *Ten* (2002).

Kiarostami takes authenticity a stage further than the neo-realists, all but dispensing with 'plot' to focus on real people doing real things in actual locations in 'real time'. He uses a minimal crew and mostly eschews a score, stripping away artifice to the point where his fiction intersects with *cinéma verité* (see page 53).

In the non-fiction narrative feature, *Close-Up* (1989), Sabzian, an illiterate film buff who passed himself off as the Iranian film-maker Mohsen Makhmalbaf, plays himself in reconstructions of his fraud. His trial is genuine documentary footage, and then Kiarostami films him meeting the real Mahkmalbaf for the first time, an encounter that may be real and scripted at the same time.

Kiarostami's most characteristic sequence is a conversation within a moving car, filmed from a single, fixed camera position. This is the dominant shot schema in the Palme d'Or winner *The Taste of Cherry* (1997), in which a man drives around offering lifts to hikers until he finds one who will comply with an unusual request. *Ten* consists of ten shots, each approximately ten minutes long, featuring either the driver or her passengers as she drives around Tehran. Despite this extreme formalism, Kiarostami's films speak profoundly to philosophical questions about love and death, and about the tensions running through Iranian society.

Ahmed Ahmed Poor as the child protagonist in Kiarostami's Where is the Friend's Home? *(1987).*

BOLLYWOOD AND HONG KONG

Although Hollywood dominates Western histories of cinema and accrued substantial dividends as the US extended its sphere of influence around the globe, the biggest national film industry isn't based in California. That distinction belongs to India. Hong Kong and Japan have also vied with Hollywood in terms of production and ticket sales (though not in profits).

The vagaries of film distribution being what they are, curious Western audiences get some opportunity to sample the work of outstanding international directors (Taiwan's Hou Hsiao-hsien, for example, or China's Zhang Yimou) while indigenous popular cinema remains uncharted territory.

For 80 years, Indian cinema has dominated its own domestic market – it currently attracts a billion ticket buyers every three months, 95 per cent of the local audience. On top of that, Indian films are at least as popular as Hollywood pictures across wide swathes of North Africa, the Middle East and Southeast Asia – and have been for decades. (Raj Kapoor's *The Vagabond – Awaara –* was reportedly seen by 65 million Russians in 1954.) In a typical year, the subcontinent will produce between 800 and 900 films, three times as many as Hollywood (and as far back as the 1920s, India was already producing more films than Great Britain).

Strictly speaking, the popular term 'Bollywood' should be reserved for Hindi films, which are made in Mumbai. Indian cinema also encompasses significant numbers of films made for Tamil speakers, Teluga, Kannada, Malyalam, Bengali, Marathi and Oriya.

Despite this diversity, commercial Indian films stick to the same formula: they are predominantly sentimental melodramas with half a dozen songs and usually three dance numbers interspersed and integrated into the story. They are relatively chaste (they pass through the same strict central censorship board). And they're long, often more than three hours.

In the fertile middle ground between the state-sponsored art cinema of Satyajit Ray, Mrinal Sen and Ritwik Ghatak, and popular escapism, we find several rewarding melodramas like Mehboob Khan's *Mother India* and Guru Dutt's *Pyaasa* (both 1957). As in other commercial cinemas, stars are the main attraction, but uniquely, songs are also a crucial selling point of all mainstream films.

There is virtually no tradition of the 'art' film in the Hong Kong film industry, at least before the emergence of the 1980s new-wave directors Wong Kar-Wai, Ann Hui and Stanley Kwan. Again, though, there is clear artistry in mainstream entertainments like King Hu's balletic wuxia (martial arts) film, *A Touch of Zen* (1970) or John Woo's romantic gunplay thriller *A Better Tomorrow* (1986).

Low budget by Hollywood standards (less than US $5 million/£3.2 million) Hong Kong action films and comedies have proved popular throughout East Asia, and unlike the commercial Indian films, which have rarely been picked up outside the diaspora, they have also achieved some popularity in the West, most notably in the case of kung-fu masters Bruce Lee in the 1970s and Jackie Chan in the 1980s and 1990s. Woo is one of a number of action directors who were lured to Hollywood prior to Hong Kong's return to Chinese sovereignty in 1996, a tacit recognition that Hollywood had lost its edge in this department.

> 'Every once in a while comes a motion picture which helps the industry to cover the mile to the milestone.'
>
> *Filmfare* magazine on *Mother India*

Sadly most Hollywood imports lose their individuality in the system. The healthy cross-fertilisation of cinematic modes that occurred naturally in the silent era (when there were no language barriers), and in the late 1960s (when the new wave had an impact almost everywhere), has fallen prey to the ubiquity of the Hollywood blockbuster in recent years, and the films are worse for it.

Wong Kar-Wai

Hong Kong director, Wong Kar-Wai, carved a niche for himself creating moody, experimental art films utilising the local industry's top stars. Wong's films work jazzy variations on his favourite theme, the romantic reverie. Despite his obsession with the past, bold, innovative aesthetic conceits and postmodern tropes mark Wong as an original.

Born 1956, Shanghai, China
Importance Leading Chinese director of the postmodern era

A former screenwriter, Wong turned director with the low-life gangster film *As Tears Go By* (1988), a Hong Kong riff on *Mean Streets*, and his most generic, least interesting film. A cut above the usual Hong Kong action melodrama all the same, it earned ten Hong Kong film award nominations and an invitation to Cannes, thus paving the ground for the swooningly romantic *Days of Being Wild* (1990), Wong's first collaboration with cinematographer Chris Doyle, and a huge step forward for the director.

Set in 1960, in the milieu Wong grew up in, *Days of Being Wild* envelops

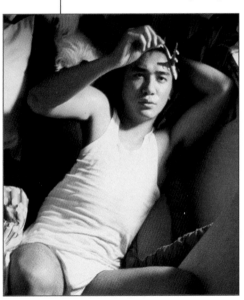

Despite being one of his smaller films, it was Chungking Express *(left) that made Wong's name in the West.*

the viewer in a half-remembered world suffused in sweltering heat, torrential rain and existential ennui. The atmosphere of longing and regret permeates almost all of Wong's films, including the all-star wuxia epic, *Ashes of Time* (1994), a dense, beguiling meditation on remembrance and forgetting, with a sometimes bewilderingly complex multilayered narrative.

In contrast, the following year's *Chungking Express* was a fast, fluid, almost throwaway picture set in contemporary Hong Kong, and comprising two simple, short, story-like through-lines. After the studied inertia of the previous two films, *Chungking Express* is a frenetic visual blur that's been likened to an action painting. Still the prevailing tone is wistful melancholy.

Happy Together (1997), which won the Best Director Prize at the Cannes Film Festival, was another radical aesthetic departure. Very much a film made in exile, *Happy Together* is shot in grainy monochrome and bluesy greens and reds, and dispenses with much of the wide-angle gimmickry. It's the most unlikely film from a former scriptwriter, which throws away the prosaic rationales of acts and arcs in favour of something more fragmented, something more akin to flicking through a photo album. This fragmentary, intuitive style carries a powerful emotional charge.

Wong spent two years obsessively shooting and reshooting *In the Mood for Love* (2000), and longer still on *2046* (2004). They share intoxicatingly seductive visuals; a poetic voice-over narration wrapped over elliptical, tentative love stories; and cyclical, repetitious structures and motifs that reverberate with Wong's previous films, going all the way back to *Days of Being Wild*.

WUXIA

This Chinese chivalric genre has its roots in ancient literature and dates back centuries. The stories are heroic legends, and have elements in common with the Japanese samurai tradition.

Jia Zhangke

China's revered director, Jia Zhangke, has chronicled the great changes that have overtaken that country over the last two or three decades, and the impact on its citizens. Because this is also the story of globalisation and accelerated capitalism, his films speak of a universal experience.

Born 1970, Shanxi, China
Importance The most important director in China at the turn of the millennium

Jia was born in 1970, in the Chinese province of Shanxi. In his lifetime, Jia has seen this rural backwater transform from an agrarian society with nineteenth-century living conditions. Twenty-first century capitalism has flooded in, bringing with it electricity, global telecommunications, highways and skyscrapers – and erasing an ancient way of life.

This transformation is the bedrock of Jia's film-making, which in indebted to Italian neo-realism in its preoccupation with working-class life, patiently observed and carefully situated in a specific time and place. Jia's minimalist aesthetic is more rigorous and demanding than that of the neo-realists, especially in the early films, which largely consist of a single, immobile take per scene. *Platform* – which traces the evolution of a cultural entertainment troupe from 1979 to 1989 (and from Maoist propaganda to synth pop) – lasts 193 minutes and has an Average Shot Length (ASL) of 68 seconds.

With international exposure, Jia has gradually moved towards a more fluid style – *The World* (*Shijie*, 2004) opens with a long, maze-like travelling shot and includes surreal animated inserts – but the ASL is still nearly a minute (57 seconds per shot). This long-take style isn't unique to Jia, but it is especially appropriate to him because time, progress and loss are central themes. In *Platform* (2000), for instance, it may feel as if nothing is happening for long periods, yet by the end we understand the world has changed.

Shanxi was also the setting for Jia's first, quasi-underground films, which included Xiao Wu *(Pickpocket, 1997), above.*

There are passages in *Still Life* (2006) that are almost indistinguishable from scenes in *Dong*, the documentary he made in the same place and at the same time. Similarly *24 City* (2008) begins as a documentary about the closure of the massive Factory 420 in Chengdu, but it incorporates 'interviews' with actors playing real people. It isn't easy to say where the reality ends and fiction takes over.

Jia combines these attributes with an uncanny intuition for the resonant metaphor. *Unknown Pleasures* (2002) literally takes its young runaway lovers to the end of the road (a highway still under construction). *The World* is set in a Vegas-style theme park where you can climb the Eiffel tower, admire the Taj Mahal and still see the World Trade Center, all without leaving Beijing. And *Still Life* is set in Fengjie, near the site of the Three Gorges dam on the Yangtze. This is one of the most celebrated locations in China but what we see is a town dismantled, brick by brick, in anticipation of the reservoir that will result when phase three of the dam is complete. It's a stunningly concrete metaphor for social impermanence.

Sam Peckinpah

A controversial figure in his lifetime, credited (or blamed) for the turn to graphic violence that overtook American film in the 1970s, Sam Peckinpah is now held in far higher esteem as the great elegist of the West, and a tough, challenging artist who put his demons on the screen.

Born 1925, Fresno, California, United States
Importance First of a new breed of directors willing to shatter the 'American Dream'
Died 1984, Inglewood, California, United States

In the 1960s and 1970s, Americans who had grown up on Hollywood movies started making their own films. Reflecting the more divisive spirit of the times, including the unpopular war in Vietnam, the struggle for civil liberties and (later) the disillusionment with the Nixon presidency, these directors often put a subversive, critical stamp on genre films. Peckinpah was among the first and most influential of this new generation. His favourite genre was the western, and his first five features as director were all westerns. Yet, more than anyone, Peckinpah showed that this mythology, the tradition of the cowboy hero as dispenser of justice, had outlived its usefulness.

Already, in his second film, *Ride the High Country* (1962) the gunslingers – Randolph Scott and Joel McCrea – are old men, nostalgic for their youth, and rueful about the mercenary values that are encroaching on the land. After the ambitious, but only half-successful, Civil War epic *Major Dundee* (1965), Peckinpah came back from a period of unemployment with his masterpiece, *The Wild Bunch* (1969). The film's story of a band of outlaws getting caught up on the wrong side in the Mexican civil war was not remarkable in itself, but Peckinpah's treatment was.

'I loved westerns as a kid, and I wanted to see if they held up.'

The brutally attenuated massacres that bookend *The Wild Bunch* confronted film-goers with a violent reality they had been sheltered

Peckinpah grew up on a ranch, the grandson of a pioneer; he served his apprenticeship writing scripts for western television series in the 1950s.

from by Hollywood convention and the injunctions of a Hollywood Production Code devised nearly 40 years before. Peckinpah used slow motion, blood squibs, and multiple cameras to transform the carnage into a savage, balletic lamentation, a moment of cinematic rupture that was both shocking and cathartic.

Neutralised through overuse, this visual bombast has become the mainstay of the modern action film. But Peckinpah's work was of a different order than that of his myriad imitators. These death throes are the extreme expression of his nihilism, but they also ennoble his outsider anti-heroes, free men who come to realise that they are anachronisms in a world of automobiles and machine guns. It's important to appreciate that the power of Peckinpah's violence derives in good measure from interludes of tender melancholy, the deep-rooted camaraderie among his desperados and their yearning for a more honest, pre-capitalist age.

Paranoid, an alcoholic and a drug addict, Peckinpah fought a losing battle with producers, studios and his anger. His later work shows a precipitous decline, but *Cross of Iron* (1977) and even *The Osterman Weekend* (1983) still reflect a bitterly cynical intelligence.

Francis Coppola

A self-styled artist who became a 1970s movie mogul, Francis Coppola is responsible for the *Godfather* trilogy, *The Conversation* (1975) and *Apocalypse Now* (1979). He pioneered digital production technology at the studio he founded, Zoetrope, until bankruptcy forced him to compromise his grand ambitions. Few film-makers have seized a greater canvas or suffered such crippling public reversals.

Born 1939, Detroit, Michigan, United States
Importance Ambitious director of countercultural films

Coppola studied drama then became one of the first film school graduates at the University of California, Los Angeles (UCLA). Even so, he learned his trade elsewhere, shooting pornography films, then moving up to Roger Corman drive-in schlock (*Dementia 13*, 1963) and, eventually, a large scale MGM musical, *Finian's Rainbow* (1968). The experience only confirmed his enthusiasm for the countercultural cinema of personal expression. Coppola formed American Zoetrope in 1969 with a group of like-minded UCLA friends and acolytes, to pursue this enthusiasm. As it turned out, *The Rain People* (1969), a low-budget road movie, was Coppola's only film in this vein.

The Godfather (1972) almost never happened. Paramount shopped the project through a dozen directors before trying Coppola. He wasn't enthusiastic about Mario Puzo's blockbuster novel, but made it his own, winning the key creative battles, including the casting of Marlon Brando as Don Vito Corleone and Al Pacino as Michael, his son; getting Nino Rota to write the score; and a running time in excess of three hours.

Right from the off, a wedding scene that takes up 20 minutes of screen time, there is a scale and gravitas to *The Godfather* which distinguishes it from its generic, pulp roots. Influenced by Luchino

Visconti's weave of authenticity and operatic spectacle in *The Leopard* and *Rocco and His Brothers*, Coppola lavishes enormous care over the film's verisimilitude, plunging us into a shadowy world where business sustains itself independently of public morality, and 'the family' takes on sinister overtones. This, Coppola implies, is the chronicle of America itself over the course of the twentieth century.

An extraordinary commercial and critical success – as was the 1975 sequel – *The Godfather* signalled a paradigm shift, ushering in an era of ambitious American film-making that would flourish until the 1980s. Ironically it also propelled Coppola away from the small-scale 'personal' films he had espoused.

A difficult three years in the making, *Apocalypse Now* placed Joseph Conrad's novella *Heart of Darkness* in Vietnam to create a surreal, hallucinatory phantasmagoria of war. At the same time, Coppola expanded his plans for Zoetrope, building a state-of-the-art digital studio and signing up film-makers from Gene Kelly to Michael Powell, Jean-Luc Godard and Wim Wenders. Sadly, the studio never produced a hit, and it declared bankruptcy in 1984.

Compelled to take on commercial assignments, Coppola made several flam-boyant mainstream films with variable results (they include *The Cotton Club*, *Bram Stoker's Dracula*, and *The Godfather III*). In a further twist, Coppola retired – then amassed such a fortune with his wine business that he could afford to bankroll his own films, *Youth Without Youth* (2007) and *Tetro* (2009).

Coppola fought to have Marlon Brando cast in The Godfather *(1972), despite Paramount preferring Laurence Olivier.*

STARS

Stars are the currency of the film business. It is difficult to attract financing without the participation of an actor, or actors, with a proven commercial track record. In addition to his or her perceived talents and attributes, the star is a guarantor of production value, and often an indication of the nature of the story.

In the first decade of the motion-picture industry, producers resisted giving billing to actors, fearing that this would give them unhealthy bargaining powers. For their part, deprived of their voices on screen, actors did not overly protest. Nevertheless, audiences were quick to single out their favourites, identifying, for example, 'The Biograph Girl', or 'The Vitagraph Girl'. An independent producer, Carl Laemmle, broke the embargo, in 1910, when he lured Florence Lawrence, the Biograph Girl, away from Biograph. To capitalise on this coup, he planted a fake story in the press denying non-existent rumours of her death – turning Florence Lawrence into a legitimate attraction in her own right. Other independent producers followed suit. Fan magazines started shortly afterwards (circa 1912), and by the end of the decade celebrity culture – or 'glamour' – was virtually synonymous with the movies.

> 'Hollywood always wanted me to be pretty, but I fought for realism.'
>
> Bette Davis

Film stars did demand more money, but their careers were at the mercy of the studios, who signed promising talent up to long-term (seven-year) contracts. Young actors were painstakingly groomed for stardom. They were coached in fencing, riding, dancing, singing and any other skills required of a matinee idol, dressed in the height of fashion, and often paired off with suitable dates, all at the studios' expense. And, of course, they were photographed to maximum advantage, in a mise-en-scène (see page 11) that was, in a sense, constructed entirely around their persona. Even so, the moguls were more than happy to suspend uncooperative stars – or punish them with inferior assignments.

In February 1919, Charlie Chaplin, Douglas Fairbanks, Mary Pickford, William S Hart and the director D W Griffith formed their own studio, United Artists (UA) with the avowed intention of escaping the 'mediocre productions' and 'machine-made entertainment' foisted on them by the studios, but their combined star power foundered, in part because they tended to indulge in less commercial, pet projects at UA, while continuing to work for the competition on the side. While the studio survived, the original signatories lost control before sound came in.

It was 1950 before stars gained real leverage in the industry. With the power of the studios waning, James Stewart and his agent, Lew Wasserman, negotiated the first 'back-end' deal. A free agent after returning from the war, Stewart cut his asking price to make the western *Winchester '73*. In exchange he received casting approval and a percentage of net box-office returns. The deal paid off so handsomely that other actors quickly followed suit. It wasn't only actors who benefited though. So did their agents. And it was the agents who really took over the reins of power, packaging deals around their clients, and setting Hollywood on an inflationary path from which it has yet to stray.

The implications are complex. American movies are more expensive by far than films made anywhere else in the world – the average Hollywood picture cost over $100 million (£65 million) to make and market in 2008, with a substantial cut going to the stars. But higher production values are also an inherent part of Hollywood's worldwide appeal.

Martin Scorsese

**The most respected of the so-called 'movie brat' generation of
directors who dominated Hollywood in the 1970s, Martin
Scorsese packs an encyclopedic knowledge of cinema and
prodigious technique into his long and eclectic
filmography. He is most celebrated, though, for his
nervy, ambivalent portraits of the modern
American gangster.**

Born 1942, New York,
New York, United States
Importance Champion
of the American
gangster movie

Growing up in New York's Little Italy, Scorsese seriously
considered entering the priesthood. But film was his true
passion. He has been a vociferous advocate for film preservation and
a tireless champion of innumerable directors. Scorsese's wide range of
influences – augmented by rock-and-roll heroes like the Rolling
Stones, The Who and Eric Clapton – feeds into his sensational
expressionism, which typically mixes dynamic movement with a
barrage of edits and a naturalistic performance style epitomised by his
talismanic actor, Robert De Niro. It's a new-wave idiom (and
Scorsese's first films were low-budget independent pictures) but with
the lavish production gloss afforded by Hollywood studio backing.

Consequently Scorsese often seems to stand with one foot inside
the system, and one outside. He is both a classicist and an iconoclast.
His films are at once subjective and objective, vicarious and removed.
This dualism is mirrored in the dramatic tension between the
antagonists of many Scorsese films from *Mean Streets* (1973) onwards.

Although he made a fine film from Edith Wharton's study of
repression *The Age of Innocence* (1993); a controversial and flawed,
but still engrossing, adaptation of Nikos Kazantzakis's *The Last
Temptation of Christ* (1988); and an entrancingly curious biopic about
the early life of the Dalai Lama, *Kundun* (1997), Scorsese is always
most at home among working-class Italian-Americans.

Raging Bull (1980), with De Niro gaining 25kg (55lb) to play the boxer Jake LaMotta, can be seen as the culmination of the American psycho-realist tradition inspired by Stanislavsky's Method (see page 41), as practised by Elia Kazan and Marlon Brando (LaMotta even quotes Brando's 'I coulda been a contender' speech at the end). It's a self-lacerating, tormented film about male aggression, with LaMotta as an uneducated, emotionally inarticulate working-class anti-hero. In Scorsese's virtuoso film-making – and De Niro's extraordinary performance – the boxer's anguish becomes all of ours. *GoodFellas* (1990), probably Scorsese's most popular film, is an apparently amoral, adrenaline-charged immersion into the world of a New York gangster – based on real life Mafioso Henry Hill – that runs from exultant highs to a chilling existential reckoning. *Casino* put similar characters against a backdrop of epic nullity: Las Vegas, Nevada.

Scorsese on location in The Departed *(2006), in which Matt Damon plays a gangster who has infiltrated the police force, while Leonardo DiCaprio is an undercover cop in the mob.*

Woody Allen

As writer, director, and until recently, star, Woody Allen has made nearly a film a year since 1971. As an actor his persona scarcely changes. As a film-maker he has been careful to work within modest means and his voice is always recognisable, but his career encompasses distinct phases and several artistic breakthroughs.

Born 1935, New York, New York, United States
Importance New York director and master of self-reflexive wit

A former standup comic and gag writer, Allen started writing film scripts in the mid 1960s, and directed his first film in 1969, the witty documentary-style crime parody, *Take the Money and Run*.

His first films – famously dubbed 'the early, funny ones' by an alien fan in the self-reflexive *Stardust Memories* (1980) – were little more than extended skits. This was true even of *Annie Hall* (1977), though this Academy Award-winning critical favourite marked the first time Allen

Allen has described Annie Hall *(left) as 'a major turning point' in his career, as he moved away from his earlier, zany comedies.*

addressed relationships in a more serious way, and riffed on his home territory without recourse to excess. It was also the first time he managed to create a romantic sparring partner as engaging as he was, courtesy of Diane Keaton's delightful ditz.

Interiors (1978) and *Stardust Memories* confirmed that Allen was taking himself more seriously. The former was a ponderous chamber piece in the style of Allen's hero, Ingmar Bergman; the latter echoed Fellini's *8½*. Neither was well received but *Manhattan* (1979) developed the mature character-based comedic style suggested by *Annie Hall*.

In the 1980s Allen found a new muse in the actress Mia Farrow. She became the centre of Allen's films, enabling him to access a much wider emotional range. Their dozen films together (plus an episode in the omnibus

> *'For some reason I'm more appreciated in France than I am back home. The subtitles must be incredibly good.'*

New York Stories) are typically modest in scale. Only three of them are longer than 90 minutes. Yet each explores an imaginative conceit with wry wit and sensitivity, teasing out philosophical ideas, ethical quandaries and emotional epiphanies.

This fecund creative period also produced *Hannah and Her Sisters* (1986), an ensemble piece as fluent and romantic as *Manhattan*. But it didn't last. As Allen's relationship with Farrow cooled (it would end in scandal when he took up with her adopted daughter) so did the films. *Husbands and Wives* (1992) is a brilliant but pitiless dissection of middle-age insecurity and infidelity, shot with a nauseatingly hand-held camera. It may be his most honest film.

Allen has kept up the pace since the scandal, apparently undeterred by the loss of several long-term collaborators. Too many of his later films feel either slapdash or overly schematic, and he's been guilty of recycling old ideas. Occasionally, though, he stills shows flashes of inspiration, even as late as *Vicky Cristina Barcelona* (2008).

Terrence Malick

With just four films as director in a career that begins in the early 1970s (a fifth is scheduled for release in 2010), Terrence Malick is almost a mythical figure in modern American film. Although he started as a screenwriter, his films play against narrative tension; they're languorous and evocative, ruminative and philosophical.

Born 1943, Ottawa, Illinois
Importance Reclusive director of films with powerful poetic overtones

Malick was brought up in Oklahoma and Texas. He got a degree in philosophy from Harvard, and received a Rhodes scholarship to Oxford, but dropped out before completing his thesis on German philosopher, Martin Heidegger. He taught philosophy at Massachusetts Institute of Technology (MIT) for a year, then enrolled in a film class at the American Film Institute.

His first feature as writer-director, *Badlands* (1973) was an independent production based on the Charles Starkweather killing spree of 1959, and thus loosely aligned with 'couple-on-the-run' films like *They Live By Night* and *Bonnie and Clyde*. But as the title implies, the plains of South Dakota and Montana dominate the action. Against this vast expanse of nothing, trigger-happy runaways Kit (Martin Sheen) and his teenage girlfirend Holly (Sissy Spacek) seem small and remote. And Malick allows them to stay that way.

Badlands remains singular for its intimate distance, the push and pull of Holly's pragmatic-romantic narration and Kit's casual violence. Laconic and poetic, this may be Malick's most completely satisfying film, even if it prefigures progressively richer and more ambitious undertakings. Few films are tuned so acutely into the wide-open spaces inside.

Five years later, he emerged with an unlikely masterpiece. A melodrama pared back to the bone and filtered through the hazy consciousness of a child, *Days of Heaven* (1978) would seem fundamentally miscast and underwritten. The production was riven with difficulties: the director maddeningly inarticulate, the cinematographer, Nestor Almendros, left halfway through, and Malick unpicked and overwrote his film during a 12-month editing process. And yet we're left with pure poetry, at once the most evocative and resonant portrait of an agrarian way of life in the early-twentieth century, and a pastoral that shades into Old Testament myth.

Malick dropped out of the limelight in the late 1970s, living as a recluse in Paris. There was no reason to believe he'd ever make

Martin Sheen and Sissy Spacek play teenage lovers on the run following a killing spree in Malick's Badlands.

another film, but 20 years later he did. An adaptation of James Jones' autobiographical novel about Guadalcanal, *The Thin Red Line* (1978) is a lyrical, meditative war film, a philosophical discourse on war. It's flawed but remarkable for the extraordinary suffusion in the natural world; the rapt poetic voice-overs; and the inspired notion of using interior monologues for soldiers on both sides of the battle lines.

The New World (2005) is no less ambitious or oblique in the way it explores the culture clash between the first European traders and Native American tribes. This, too, is a kind of Eden story, conveyed through rhapsodic imagery and multiple interior monologues.

Steven Spielberg

A brilliant craftsman with an intuitive sense of what the film-going public wants to see, Steven Spielberg is one of the most successful directors in the history of Hollywood. He has brought wonder and warmth to blockbuster entertainments like *ET* (1982), and occasionally stretched the mainstream with *Schindler's List* (1993) and *Saving Private Ryan* (1998).

Born 1946, Cincinnati, Ohio, United States
Importance A master of the blockbuster movie

After some two-dozen films as director, and many more as producer, it's clear where Spielberg's interests lie: science fantasy, history, race and the Jewish identity, family, childhood and escapism.

Like Hitchcock, Spielberg storyboards his films frame by frame. And, like Hitchcock, he sees the director's primary function as playing the audience's emotions. Early breakthroughs *Duel* (1971) and *Jaws* (1975) are mechanical exercises in suspense and fear. But with *Close Encounters of the Third Kind* (1977) he revealed a more optimistic sensibility, one that thrilled in imagining benevolent alien life forms and a better world somewhere beyond our own. By the time he made *ET: The Extra-Terrestrial*, Disney seemed to be a

At the time of its release, in 1982,
ET *was the biggest-selling film of all time.*

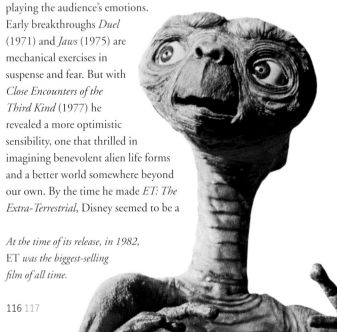

more important reference point than Hitchcock, with a special empathy for childlike wonder, and the innocence and vulnerability that it implies.

Yet Spielberg has always conducted his career with an eye on the bottom line. When Universal booked *Jaws* onto 400 screens and bought unprecedented television advertising at the height of summer, pushing the box-office to $100 million within weeks, the blockbuster era was born. Spielberg and *Star Wars* creator, George Lucas, drove this business model, racking up half a dozen of the biggest hits ever made between them. While other film-makers reworked classical genres to fashion a more contemporary, often cynical perspective, Spielberg and Lucas dressed up old B-movie staples like the Saturday adventure serial in state-of-the-art special effects and big- budget production values.

By the mid 1980s Spielberg was able to do any film he chose. He made expert adaptations of worthy literary sources, Alice Walker's *The Color Purple* (about slavery); J G Ballard's autobiographical novel about internment in Japan during the Second World War, *Empire of the Sun*; and Thomas Kenneally's *Schindler's List*, about the Holocaust. But if he craved respect, he still wanted to be loved: the serious films are marred by sentimentality, and interspersed with the likes of *Hook* (1991), *Jurassic Park* (1993) and further instalments of Indiana Jones (1981; 1984; 1989; 2008).

> **SATURDAY ADVENTURE SERIAL**
> Picture serials were popular in the silent era through to the 1950s, when they migrated to television. They were half-hour adventure stories, shown in weekly instalments, each ending on a cliffhanger, predominantly to a juvenile audience on Saturday mornings.

The dichotomy between earnest films and frivolous entertainments suggests that Spielberg isn't entirely comfortable with either one. *A.I.: Artificial Intelligence* (2001) is his most personal and revealing film, no matter that it started out as a Stanley Kubrick project. An existential fairytale drawing on *ET*, *Pinocchio* and *The Wizard of Oz*, *A.I.* is the story of a 'mecha-boy', a robot prototype who thinks and feels like a real boy, but who sets out to find his maker after he is rejected by his (human) parents. In this anguished tale of an orphan, for once Spielberg speaks to us equally from the head and the heart.

DIGITAL CINEMA

In its first century, the apparatus of film production remained fundamentally unchanged. The introduction of synchronous sound recording, in 1927, had a great impact, and the slow transition to colour and the anamorphic (widescreen) format altered the face of film. But digital technology, in its myriad forms, has further-reaching implications for the medium.

Digital's first incursion came in the field of special effects, when computer graphics offered an alternative to traditional animation and trick photography. The science-fiction film *Tron* (1982) was set inside a video game – but, at that point, the technology could not combine live action and computer graphics in the same frame.

That breakthrough came in the early 1990s, and was showcased in blockbusters like Spielberg's *Jurassic Park* (1993) and the Robert Zemeckis film *Forrest Gump* (1994), in which Tom Hanks shakes hands with President Kennedy and co-star Gary Sinise's legs were digitally amputated. The first completely digital feature was Pixar's computer-animation *Toy Story* (1995).

In the last 10 years, Computer Generated Imagery (CGI) has spearheaded a return to spectacle in the costume epic (*Gladiator*; *Kingdom of Heaven*); science-fiction (*Star Wars* I to III); and fantasy films (*Lord of the Rings*; *Harry Potter*; *The Chronicles of Narnia*). Sets, props, special effects, costumes, even actors… All can be added into (or removed from) a scene after it's been shot. So called 'live-action' films can become more painterly, more fantastical, more like animation and more like a virtual reality game. In *Sky Captain and the World of Tomorrow* (2004) almost everything but the actors and their costumes was created on a computer, and Jude Law shared the screen with Laurence Olivier, 'resurrected' 15 years after the latter's death.

By this time, the traditional methods of film editing had been superceded by digital, non-linear editing machines (introduced by Avid in 1989). Instead of spooling through reels of rushes and cutting physical strips of celluloid, editors could access data instantly and play around with virtual edits. This mutability extended to the film's afterlife. It was in the 1990s that studios began re-releasing library titles in a revised 'director's cut', a marketing hook that became ubiquitous as DVD – the digital virtual disc – supplanted home video. Film was no longer simply an abstract sensory experience; it could be boxed and taken home in a tangible, plastic form. Going in to the twenty-first century, the DVD market boosted studio profits so much that, by 2005, theatrical box-office grosses represented only 15 per cent of worldwide revenues, with 85 per cent coming from home entertainment (TV and DVD sales).

Digital video camera technology has improved steadily since the 1980s. Independent and low-budget film-makers began to switch to DV equipment in the late 1990s, primarily to cut costs. DV cameras were easy to use. They could shoot in low light conditions and record sound directly. There was no need to send the negative to a lab, and no expensive film stock to buy, so film-makers could afford to shoot more freely. Then they could edit at home on their computers. The autobiographical documentary *Tarnation* (2003) was edited on i-Movie and the rough cut came in on a budget of $218 (£142).

> *'I'm as guilty as anyone, because I helped to herald the digital era with* Jurassic Park. *But the danger is that it can be abused to the point where nothing is eye-popping any more.'*
>
> Steven Spielberg

In 2008, Steven Soderbergh shot his four-hour, two-part biopic *Che* using the latest High Definition system, Red. Digital distribution could theoretically reduce costs tenfold. It is easy to imagine that the days of celluloid are over.

David Cronenberg

Cerebral and visceral, David Cronenberg graduated from controversial, graphic, low-budget horror films to elegantly subversive art films. His career has gone through several distinct phases, yet his preoccupations with the body, identity, transformation and flux have remained constant.

Born 1943, Toronto, Canada
Importance A master of 'body horror' and psychological drama

A former science student, who switched his degree to literature, then made experimental underground films influenced by Andy Warhol, Cronenberg first made his name with a series of transgressive low-budget horror films, including *Shivers* (1975), *The Brood* (1979) and *Scanners* (1981). The films are characterised by shockingly visceral, even lurid, ideas – sexual contagion, exploding heads – made manifest in a matter-of-fact, almost antiseptic style. The term 'body horror' describes these forays into genetic mutation, physical repulsion and psychic damage, which culminated in *Videodrome* (1983), a witty psycho-fantasy about viral-image contamination inspired by the director's censorious critics.

The same year, Cronenberg quit Canada for Hollywood to make Stephen King's *The Dead Zone*, probably his most anonymous effort, and certainly his safest (he wouldn't take a script credit again until *eXistenZ* in 1999). But *The Fly* (1986) proved he hadn't mellowed. This remake of a 1958 Vincent Price film featured stomach-churning, gross-out effects. A tragicomic parable about genetic mutation, it is also a heartbreaking love story, in which the connection between man and woman (Jeff Goldblum and Geena Davis) is more important than man and insect. It remains his biggest hit.

Dead Ringers (1988) is another masterpiece, a devastating psychological drama about identical twins (Jeremy Irons). By now Cronenberg's key collaborative team was firmly in place and the

David Cronenberg on the set of A History of Violence *(2005) with actor Viggo Mortenson, who also took the main role in* Eastern Promises *(2007).*

wooden performances from his low-budget pictures were succeeded by compelling work by the likes of Goldblum and Irons. He began to look further afield for inspiration: to Burroughs for *Naked Lunch* (1991), playwright David Henry Hwang for *M Butterfly* (1993), J G Ballard for *Crash* (1996). Cronenberg had escaped from the horror ghetto to make what are essentially art films, albeit marked with his abiding fascination with 'altered states' – those moments when we are liberated from, or transcend, the physical confines of the body. *Crash* is probably the best film of this period, though its semi-comic, nihilistic view of perpetual sexual frustration proved controversial.

A History of Violence (2005) and *Eastern Promises* (2007) seem to mark another departure: conventional thrillers on the surface, both ask provocative questions about Viggo Mortensen's characters: to what extent is his capacity for violence heroic? Can the assumption of virtue not only disguise, but also redeem our sins – or vice versa? In other words, when do we cease to be ourselves? Cronenberg himself seems immune to that question: his DNA is all over these pictures.

David Lynch

David Lynch has made some of the strangest and most disturbing films ever created. A pop surrealist, he has enjoyed conspicuous success in the mainstream despite the ambiguity, perversity and violence at the heart of his vision. Quirky, deadpan humour and a luscious visual palette complete the picture.

Born 1946, Missoula, Montana, United States
Importance Creator of dark, shadowy, unsettling films

David Lynch was the son of an agricultural scientist – hence, perhaps, the famous opening sequence of *Blue Velvet* (1986), which takes us from a kitsch vision of small-town Americana (white picket fences, red roses, brilliant blue sky) only to dive into a tenebrous undergrowth.

Lynch came to film from painting. His first short films (*The Alphabet*, 1967; *The Grandmother*, 1970) were experimental mixtures of live-action and stop-motion animation, kinetic sculptures with tortured adolescent heroes entering a dark, putrid world. His first feature, shot on an art grant over five years, *Eraserhead* (1976) is a clear evolution of this early work, with a gallery of grotesques trapped in a nightmarish urban wasteland. Filmed in high-contrast black and white, with a cacophonous industrial soundtrack and stark, decrepit design, it reeks of alienation, sexual revulsion and domestic horror.

This led to an offer to direct *The Elephant Man* (1980), the true story of Victorian circus freak, John Merrick, (played by John Hurt), 'saved' by a philanthropic doctor and adopted by polite society. Lynch turned Dickensian London into a feverish, infernal environment where the normal and the monstrous can switch places. *The Elephant Man* was widely praised and nominated for eight Academy Awards.

Following the expensive flop *Dune* (1984), Lynch was allowed to make his own original script, *Blue Velvet*, without interference. A disquieting blend of anodyne teen film and toxic noir, the film is a

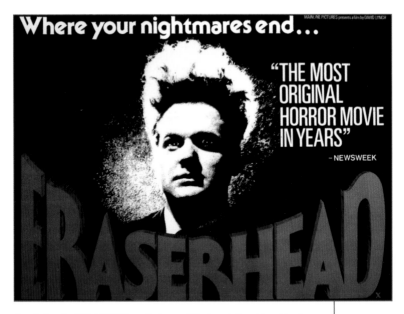

Lynch described his 1976 film as 'a dream of dark and disturbing things'.

subversive pop artifice and an Oedipal nightmare; its knowing, postmodern ambiance punctured with shocking eruptions of violent sex and narcotic delirium.

Similar juxtapositions wind their way through *Wild at Heart* (1990) and *Twin Peaks*, the alternately kooky and ominous television series that became a surprise hit in 1990. The underrated film spin-off, *Twin Peaks: Fire Walk With Me* (1992) upped the ante with a shift away from closed narrative towards the more enigmatic surrealist strategies that make *Lost Highway* (1997), *Mulholland Dr.* (2001) and *Inland Empire* (2006) fascinating but perplexing experiences. Multiple viewing is required to explore (but not explain) the mysteries of these later films. The latter two both have self-reflexive Hollywood settings, and Lynch seems increasingly drawn to investigate the psychic damage that accrues in and around the dream factory.

Spike Lee

An exuberant storyteller and dedicated social commentator, Spike Lee is one of the more prolific and successful of the film-school graduates who came up in the 1980s and carved out a space for themselves in the mainstream. The most prominent African-American film-maker to date, he has embraced the roles of spokesperson, entrepreneur and role model.

Born 1957, Atlanta, Georgia, United States
Importance Leading African-American film-maker

Lee isn't the first African-American director. Significant trailblazers include Oscar Michaux, who made more than two-dozen films primarily for the 'coloured' market between 1919 and 1948; Gordon Parks, who directed *Shaft* (1971); Melvin van Peebles, Sidney Poitier and Charles Burnett. Nevertheless, Lee is unique for staying true to his concerns while reaching a wide, multiracial audience.

A contemporary of Joel Coen and Ang Lee, Lee went to film school in the early 1980s (New York University's Tisch School of the Arts) and raised independent finance for his first feature: *She's Gotta Have It* (1986). A black-and-white comedy about a promiscuous New Yorker juggling four boyfriends, the film had a new-wave, screwball vibe, with lots of flashy jump cuts and giddy camera moves. Shot for $175,000, it went on to make $7 million in North America alone.

School Daze (1988) was a misfire, but everything came together with his third film, *Do the Right Thing* (1989). Set over the course of a sweltering summer day in Bed-Stuy, New York, the film follows Mookie, a pizza-delivery boy (played by Lee), who encounters a cross-section of the community: various black and Latino youths, their elders (Ossie Davies and Ruby Dee), and Mookie's Italian-American employers at the pizzeria, Sal (Danny Aiello) and his sons, the racist Pino (John Turturro) and colour-blind Vito (Richard Edson).

Shot in bold, heavily saturated colours and using a blaring rap soundtrack *Do the Right Thing* bristles with energy and purpose. The film confronts racist attitudes in various guises before magnifying the tensions in a scrappy, morally ambiguous climax. Derided as inflammatory in some quarters because Lee's character kicks off a riot in disgust at police brutality, this is vital, challenging cinema.

Subsequent 'Spike Lee Joints' include *Mo' Better Blues* (1990), *Jungle Fever* (1991), *Crooklyn* (1994), *Clockers* (1995) and *He Got Game* (1998). None of them hits the same high pitch – Lee has a tendency to throw too many balls in the air, and his bravura aesthetic choices can be needlessly distracting – but taken together, the films constitute an urgent, voluble chorus of black voices, attitudes and arguments. In addition to this, the big budget biopic *Malcolm X* (1992) is both an impressive film in its own right and a resounding political accomplishment.

Lee's success – and the rise of hip-hop and rap – spurred a wave of new black films. If the ghetto 'gangsta' films of the early 1990s fizzled out, the rising stars he fostered early on (including Wesley Snipes, Samuel L Jackson, Halle Berry and Denzel Washington) have had an enduring impact. Lee's documentaries *4 Little Girls* (1997) and *When the Levees Broke* (2006) back up his record of political engagement, while the dramas *Summer of Sam* (1999), *25th Hour* (2002) and *Inside Man* (2006) find Lee telling multiracial New York City stories with true verve and intelligence.

Spike Lee is celebrated for tackling tough issues in his films, which have dealt with politics, race relations, urban crime and poverty.

Quentin Tarantino

For many, Quentin Tarantino was the most distinctive and exciting voice to emerge in American movies in the 1990s. A pop-postmodernist and natural-born magpie, Tarantino constructs his genre hybrids from a dazzling array of international influences, rewriting the rule book as he does so.

Born 1963, Knoxville, Tennessee, United States
Importance Writer-director of controversial genre hybrids

A video-shop clerk who never went to college, Tarantino is a film nut apparently equally passionate about buxom blaxploitation queen Pam Grier as he is about Jean-Luc Godard. Coming up through the lively US independent sector of the late 1980s and early 1990s, he announced himself with the bravura crime thriller, *Reservoir Dogs* (1992), which he wrote and directed.

Beginning in the middle and carving the story of a failed diamond robbery into a series of chapters that introduces each of the gangsters by turn, Tarantino rifles through the heist movie back catalogue, borrowing from Kubrick's *The Killing*, Ringo Lam's *City on Fire*, and Jean-Pierre Melville as he sees fit, and all but omitting the robbery itself.

Tarantino's profane, funny, pop-littered dialogue puts its own ironic spin on things – his heavies don't talk like movie gangsters, they talk like geeks who have seen too many films. But it's the disquieting ease with which Tarantino jumps from postmodern cool to blood-soaked violence that made the film controversial.

His second film, *Pulp Fiction* (1994), was even more audacious in the way it scrambled the chronology of three interlocking narratives, as if in homage to

'That's part of my talent, really – putting the way people really speak into the things I write. My only obligation is to my characters. And they came from where I have been.'

Godard's observation that a story should have a beginning, a middle and an end, 'but not necessarily in that order'. Tarantino unleashed a torrent of black-comic verbal riffs and repartee. If the tone is relentlessly glib, the characters all have their own axes to grind (sometimes literally), and the momentum never flags throughout the 154-minute running time. Backed by Miramax Films, it won the Palme d'Or and broke the $100-million (£65-million) barrier at the North American box office, ushering in the era of the 'mini-major', through which the studios co-opted many of the best and brightest of the independent sector.

Jackie Brown (1997) was a more subdued crime film, based on an Elmore Leonard novel. With its graceful middle-aged protagonists played by 1970s B movie icons Pam Grier and Robert Forster, it was the first Tarantino film with characters you actually cared about.

After a long break, he returned with the two-part revenge odyssey *Kill Bill* (2003 and 2004), such a patchwork quilt of influences – comic books, Sergio Leone, manga, the Shaw Brothers, Brian De Palma – that it resembles a new form of film-making, more akin to sampling or a mash-up than traditional dramaturgy. *Deathproof* (2007), originally one half of the *Grindhouse* package, was another exercise in retro-fitting, this time giving a feminist edge to sleazy-killer car-exploitation fare.

Kill Bill *(2003) saw Tarantino reteam with Uma Thurman, whose flagging career he had previously revived with* Pulp Fiction *(1994).*

Index

For main entries see contents page. References to fashion designers are given only where mentioned other than their main entry.